MODERN indian

MODERN
indian

Rishi Desai

NEW HOLLAND

First published in 2014 by
New Holland Publishers
London · Sydney · Cape Town · Auckland
www.newhollandpublishers.com · www.newholland.com.au

The Chandlery Unit 114 50 Westminster Bridge Road London SE1 7QY
1/66 Gibbes Street Chatswood NSW 2067 Australia
Wembley Square First Floor Solan Road Gardens Cape Town 8001 South Africa
218 Lake Road Northcote Auckland New Zealand

A catalogue record of this book is available at the British Library and at the National Library of Australia

ISBN: 9781742575049

10 9 8 7 6 5 4 3 2 1

Managing director: Fiona Schultz
Publisher: Diane Ward
Project editor: Simona Hill
Designer: Tracy Loughlin
Stylist: Rhianne Contreras
Photographer: Sue Stubbs
Production director: Olga Dementiev
Printer: Toppan Leefung Printing Limited

Follow New Holland Publishers on
Facebook: www.facebook.com/NewHollandPublishers

The Publisher would like to thank the following for providing props for photography: Malcolm Greenwood
Shelley Panton, Mud and Papaya for providing ceramics, STONE for providing linens.

Contents

Introduction

Born and raised in a small town in India, food has always been part of my identity. Kolhapur, my home town may be small but has a rich cultural and food history and it's there where it all began for me. Growing up in a big family, my mother, Uma, catered for the culinary needs of 5 kids and 6 adults in the house, making sure that there was at least one meat dish to be served every day. My mother's culinary style has had a huge influence on me and my food, which has come a long way from the narrow Kolhapur streets. As I travelled from a small town to the big cities of India through North America into Australia, my repertoire evolved from spicy Indian curries to vibrant Southeast Asian food and subtle European cuisine.

My eclectic food journey has taken me to some of the most amazing places. As a child, my father introduced me to different meats while my mother, who grew up on the coast, introduced me to seafood. At home, Monday was a day off for butchers so no fresh meat was available. My father would either stock up a day in advance, or my mother would go to the fishmonger for fresh fish instead. She would prepare Kolhapuri goat curry or fry a whole fish, and while my siblings were squabbling for the most tender pieces of meat or fish, I would happily savour goat's liver and fish head. I would go in the kitchen and watch my mother prepare the food, and I would taste every curry paste she made and absorbed every technique she used. My mother has a spice shop and she makes her own spice blends from scratch. She taught me how to make them and helped me to understand the variety of meats and produce that combine best with each. While my friends were playing cricket, I would be trying my hand at replicating recipes in the kitchen.

This hobby served me well when I moved away from home to study at university. I had a new city to explore, new foods to try and friends to make. Food helped me forge new connections quickly and easily. The university town was more cosmopolitan than my home town and was my first tryst with French, Italian and Asian cuisines.

My degree took me to North America and that's where my eyes were really opened up to the world of International cuisine. I wandered the streets of New York City to find the famous New York peperoni pizza or that tasty Greek gyro I'd heard all about. I got to experience the wonder of Chinatown and from those visits Chinese food became my cuisine of choice.

My vocation took me to Australia in 2008 and my new found love for food turned into an obsession. I instantly fell in love with the Aussie barbie and the concept of going to the beach to eat fish and chips. I was amazed by the number of Asian restaurants and the variety of Asian food that I could get my hands on. I discovered the real meaning of fresh produce and a truly amazing variety of seafood.

Every now and then though I'd get the urge to go back to my roots and crave Indian curry. I looked for the flavours I grew up with and savoured but would often end up disappointed with the choices available. Indian food is much more than just curries to me. India is a land of much splendour with diversity in its people, language and food. The spices and cooking methods change astonishingly across the regions resulting in unique flavours.

The recipes I have incorporated in this book showcase the diversity of Indian food and features my contemporary take on traditional recipes. It's a collection of 70 eclectic dishes that originate from different parts of India. I have included the basics to get you started, reinvented some classics and incorporated some innovative ideas incorporating contemporary cooking techniques for the adventurous. The key element is to retain the traditional flavours.

Spices form an integral part of Indian food so the book begins with some basic spice blends that you can create and store at home. Commonly used spice blends such as garam masala and versatile curry powder are essential in any Indian pantry. Most homes will have their own blend of these masalas. The spice blends featured in this book have been passed on in my family for generations. These blends are incorporated in the recipes that follow.

Traditionally condiments such as pickles and relishes were prepared in large quantities in India when the fruits were in season and stored for the rest of the year. Now that most fruits are available all year around, they need not be made in large quantities. I've included recipes for small portions of popular condiments such as mango or lemon relish. These condiments go well with any or all meals and are just as good with a piece of toast.

When you think of Indian food the things that come to mind are spicy curries, flat breads, rice and sweets. The range of Indian breads available originate from the different regions of India. No Indian cookbook would be complete without them. The dough used to make these breads are as versatile as the breads themselves and can be stuffed, pan-fried or deep-fried to make parathas, flat breads or puris.

I've also included my take on popular Indian street-foods, reinterpreting them and presenting them with an elegance. Pani Puri, Chaat, Bhel and Wada Pav are popular foods on the streets of India. Their lingering aroma compels you to stop by the roadside vendor to grab a bite.

There are some gems too – native recipes that are yet to be explored outside of the region of their origin. The recipes such as Malabar fish, Mangalore Squid, Chicken Cafreal and Chettinad Chicken use spice blends that are not commonly found outside India. Slow-cooked Kolhapuri Goat is an ode to my home town Kolhapur. Coconut Milk Poached Salmon and Biryani are my personal favourites.

I've included an interesting collection of vegetarian recipes too, such as Vegetarian Sliders, the artistic and amusing Vegetable Garden, Onion Fritters and quesdilla-inspired Potato Parathas, just to name a few.

From the plethora of Indian sweets available I've selected the most popular and presented my contemporary take on them. Classics such as Gulab Jamun, Semolina Halwa and Rice Pudding have been revitalised to give them a different dimension. Then there's the Guava Pudding and Mum's Trifle, which nod to nostalgia.

Rishi Desai

Twitter: @rishidesaii
Instagram: RISHIDESAII

The Essentials

Can you imagine Indian food without spices?

I certainly can't! Spices are the hallmarks of Indian food. Every household has its own special spice blend or 'masala' made to a recipe handed down from cook to cook. I've included the most popular blends here. Make them up and store them in the refrigerator so that you have a ready supply to hand. They are incomparable to any shop bought item.

The Essentials section wouldn't be complete without recipes for fluffy naan breads, chapatis and rotis, which offer a light and quick means to scoop up curries. Equally important to any dish is the rice accompaniment.

Garam Masala

Garam masala is a very versatile and essential ingredient in a lot of Indian recipes. This recipe was passed to me by my mother. Use it in curries and dal.

Garam masala will stay fresh for up to 3 months.
Preparation time: 5 minutes / Cooking time: 10 minutes

500 g (1 lb 2 oz) coriander seeds
10 g (⅓ oz) cloves
10 g (⅓ oz) cinnamon quills (sticks)
10 g (⅓ oz) black cardamom
10 g (⅓ oz) cumin seeds
10 g (⅓ oz) black peppercorns
50 g (1¾ oz) fennel seeds
50 g (1¾ oz) poppy seeds
5 g (⅙ oz) ground nutmeg powder
2 bay leaves

In a frying pan, over medium heat, roast all of the spices for 3 minutes.

Blend to a fine powder in a blender or using a coffee grinder. Sift through a fine mesh.

Store in an airtight container in the freezer.

Tandoori Spice Mix

This is an ideal spice blend for an open-fire barbeque. Combine with yogurt or lemon juice, then use to coat any meat, seafood or even vegetables. In North India it is used in Butter Chicken and Chicken Tikka Masala.

Tandoori spice mix will stay fresh for up to 3 months.
Preparation time: 5 minutes / Cooking time: 10 minutes

1 tablespoon ground coriander
1 tablespoon ground cumin
1 teaspoon red chilli powder
1 tablespoon ground ginger
1 tablespoon dried garlic or garlic granules
⅛ teaspoon of salt

Combine all the ingredients in a blender and blend to a fine powder.

Store in an airtight container.

Basic All-In-One Masala (Curry Powder)

'Curry powder' is very popular in the western world but this name is rarely used in India for the spice mix. Instead it is commonly known as sambar powder, which originates in south India. Use it to make Sambar.

Curry powder will stay fresh for up to 3 months.
Preparation time: 5 minutes / Cooking time: 10 minutes

2 teaspoon coriander seeds
2 teaspoon cumin seeds
2 cloves
2 cardamom pods
1 teaspoon fenugreek seeds
4 black peppercorns
½ dry red chilli
½ teaspoon garlic flakes
¼ teaspoon ginger powder
½ teaspoon turmeric

In a frying pan, over medium heat, roast the coriander seeds, cumin seeds, cloves, cardamom, fenugreek seeds, peppercorns and red chilli for 3 minutes or until fragrant.

In a blender, add all the roasted spices and combine them with the garlic flakes, ginger powder and turmeric and blend to fine powder.

Panchphoron Spice Mix

Panchphoron is a traditional Bengali Eastern Indian spice mix. Add the mix to a little oil in a hot pan and sauté for 20 seconds or so before adding other ingredients. Use it to add a different dimension to a curry.

Panchphoron spice mix will stay fresh for up to 3 months
Preparation time: 5 minutes

75 g/2½ oz/½ cup nigella seeds
75 g/2½ oz/½ cup cumin seeds
75 g/2½ oz/½ cup black mustard seeds
75 g/2½ oz/½ cup fenugreek seeds
75 g/2½ oz/½ cup fennel seeds

Mix all the ingredients together and keep in an airtight container.

Ghee

Ghee, or clarified butter, is used extensively in Indian cooking because it tastes so much better than regular vegetable oil. It has a higher smoking point than oil and contains less milk solids than butter meaning that you can heat ghee to a much higher temperature than butter. Buy ghee in the supermarket, or use this recipe to make it for half the price.

Cooking time: 25 minutes

450 g (1 lb) unsalted butter

Melt the butter in a heavy pan over low heat. Simmer until all the milk solids become golden brown and settle at the base of the pan, about 25–30 minutes. Be careful not to burn the milk solids. Strain the ghee and store in an airtight container. Use it in place of oil.

Basmati Rice (Absorption Method)

Rice fields are the first thing that come to mind when I think of Asia. Southeast Asia, China and the southern subcontinent are famous for sticky rice, while in the northern part of the subcontinent, fluffy aromatic basmati rice is more prevalent. This absorption method will result in sticky rice, which is perfect with sweet-and-sour sambar.

Serves: 4 / Preparation time: 5 minutes
Cooking time: 20 minutes

200 g/7 oz/1 cup basmati rice
½ teaspoon salt
475 ml/16 fl oz/2 cups of water

Add the rice, salt and water to a large saucepan or rice cooker. Bring to the boil and boil on medium heat for 15 minutes, or until the rice is cooked through. Add more water, if necessary.

Boiled Basmati Rice

The boiling method of cooking rice results in aromatic fluffy basmati rice, which is perfect to serve with curries from the northern subcontinent. This rice is also ideal for making different pulao (pilaf).

Serves: 4 / Preparation time: 5 minutes
Cooking time: 20 minutes

1.5 litres/2½ pints/6 cups water
200 g/7 oz/1 cup basmati rice
½ teaspoon salt

In a rice cooker or a saucepan, add water, rice and salt. Boil according to the packet instructions until the rice is cooked through. Strain the excess water and leave the rice to cool. Cooling the rice makes it fluffy as moisture evaporates.

Naan Bread

Although the word 'naan' finds its origin in Persia and means 'bread', it has a more specific meaning in South Asia. This leavened flatbread is traditionally cooked in a tandoor, a clay-lined coal oven. Its fluffy, soft texture makes it the most famous and best loved Indian flatbread around the world.

Makes: 4 / Preparation time: 40 minutes
Cooking time: 10 minutes

½ teaspoon sugar
75 ml (2 fl oz/⅓ cup) warm water
3 g dried yeast
200 g (7 oz/1¾ cups) plain (all-purpose) flour, plus extra
    for dusting
¼ teaspoon salt
125 ml (4 fl oz/ ½ cup) plain (natural) yogurt
1 garlic clove
¼ teaspoon sesame seeds
¼ teaspoon butter or ghee, to serve

In a small bowl, stir together the sugar, warm water and yeast. Set aside in a warm place for 5–10 minutes, or until it froths.

In a mixing bowl, mix the flour and salt together. Make a well in the centre and add the yeast mixture and yogurt.

Turn out onto a lightly floured surface and knead until the dough is soft, about 10 minutes. Alternatively, use a food mixer with a dough hook attachment to knead the dough for 10 minutes.

Weigh 85 g (3 oz) pieces of dough and roll each into a ball. Place on a floured plate about 5 cm (2 in) apart. Cover with a damp cloth or cling film (plastic wrap) and set aside in a warm place for at least 30 minutes, or until they double in size.

Dust the work surface with flour and using a rolling pin, roll the dough balls into elliptical or round shapes. Cover and leave to rest for 5 more minutes.

Grate (mince) garlic on top and sprinkle with sesame seeds.

Heat a frying pan and place a naan bread in the pan. Once you see some air bubbles popping up, flip it over and cook the second side. Using tongs, remove the bread from the pan and cook the first side straight on the flame until the naan puffs up. Spread butter or ghee on top and serve hot.

Roti

Cutlery doesn't come close to flat breads as a utensil for scooping up curries from a plate. It's an essential element of Indian cuisine. This light and quick roti can be used as an after-school snack for instead of bread and cookies.

Makes: 6 / Preparation time: 10 minutes
Cooking time: 15 minutes

175 g (6 oz/1½ cups) plain (all-purpose) flour, plus extra for dusting
1 teaspoon salt
20 g (¾ oz) butter, melted
175 ml (6 fl oz/¾ cup) water, chilled

Mix the flour and salt in a large bowl. Make a well in the centre and slowly add the water. Stir to bring the dough together.

Dust the work surface with some flour, turn the dough out and knead for at least 5 minutes. Cover with cling film (plastic wrap) and set aside to rest for 10 minutes.

Weigh 60 g (2 oz) of the dough and form into a ball. Dust the work surface with flour and roll out the dough into round roti using a rolling pin.

Heat a frying pan over medium heat and place the rolled roti in the pan. Once a few air bubbles are visible on the surface, check the underside to ensure it is slightly cooked. Cook the second side until it is golden brown. Remove the pan from the heat and using tongs, cook the first side on the open flame until the roti puffs up. Serve hot drizzled with butter or ghee.

Flat Bread (Chapatti)

Chapatti is made using wholemeal flour, or atta, as it is called in Hindi, and while roti is finished over an open flame, chapatti is cooked entirely in a frying pan.

Makes: 6 / Preparation time: 10 minutes
Cooking time: 15 minutes

175 g (6 oz/1½ cup) wholemeal (whole-wheat) flour/atta, plus extra for dusting
1 teaspoon salt
175 ml (6 fl oz/¾ cup) luke warm water
1 teaspoon vegetable oil
Ghee, butter or vegetable oil, to serve

Mix the flour and salt in a large bowl. Make a well in the centre and slowly add the water while mixing. Knead until the dough comes together, then add the oil and knead for another 3 minutes until soft. Cover with cling film (plastic wrap) and set aside to rest for 10 minutes.

Weigh 60 g (2 oz) of the dough and form into a ball. Dust the work surface with flour and roll out the dough into round bread using a rolling pin.

Heat a frying pan on medium heat and place the flatbread on the pan. Once a few air bubbles are visible on the flatbread turn it over making sure the first side is only slightly cooked. Cook the second side until it is golden brown. Turn once again and cook the first side until golden brown. Remove from the pan and drizzle with ghee, butter or vegetable oil. Serve hot.

Vegetable Pilaf

Pilaf and similar dishes are common to Balkan, Middle Eastern, Caucasian, Central and Southern Asian, East African, Latin American, and Caribbean cuisines. Every region has its own influence on pilaf. In India, the vegetarian version made with vibrantly coloured vegetables is loved all around the country. The balance of spices and the fragrance of basmati rice makes this dish ideal to be served with any curry.

Serves: 6 / Preparation time: 5 minutes
Cooking time: 20 minutes

2 tablespoon ghee (clarified butter)

2 green chillies, sliced

2 black cardamom pods

4 green cardamom pods

2 cinnamon quills (sticks)

6 cloves

10 black peppercorns

2 bay leaves

400 g/14 oz/2 cups basmati rice

115 g (4 oz/1 cup) frozen mixed vegetables (peas, carrots, corn)

1 teaspoon salt

2 teaspoons fried shallots, to garnish

In a saucepan heat the ghee over medium heat, then sauté the green chillies, black and green cardamom, cinnamon, cloves, black peppercorns and bay leaves for 30 seconds. Add the rice and sauté for 2 minutes until fragrant.

Transfer to a rice cooker with 1 litre (1¾ pints/ 4 cups) water, the frozen vegetables and salt, and cook as per rice cooker instructions. If you don't have a rice cooker, use the absorption method to cook the rice. Garnish with fried shallots.

Rice and Urid Dal Crêpes (Dosai)

Dosai are South Indian crêpes that are very popular. I learnt to make perfect dosai when I was living in Bangalore (a South Indian metro city). Dosai requires natural fermentation of the batter, which can be a bit tricky if you live in colder climates. Keep the batter in a warm place to aid the fermentation process. These crispy golden brown dosai are best served with curried potato or sambar.

Preparation time: At least 1 day / Cooking time: 10 minutes

400 g (14 oz/2 cups) rice
200 g (7 oz/1 cup) white urid dal or white lentils
½ teaspoon salt
1 teaspoon oil per dosa
Ghee, to serve

Soak the rice and urid dal separately in warm water overnight.

Finely purée the rice and urid dal separately in a food processor, adding a small quantity of water, if necessary until a smooth consistency.

Mix the purées together in a metal or glass bowl, cover with a lid and leave in a warm, dry place to ferment for at least 12 hours. It should double in size when the fermentation is complete.

Mix the salt into the batter with just enough water to create a consistency similar to crêpe batter.

Heat a heavy non-stick frying pan and drizzle in a small amount of oil. Make sure the oil coats the entire pan. Pour a cup of mixture in the middle of the pan and using the small flat base of a cup or glass spread the batter over the entire pan base.

Alternatively, swirl the pan quickly to spread the batter on the pan to coat evenly. Cook over medium heat on one side only until golden brown and crispy. Drizzle with ghee once you see the edges of the crêpes start to peel off the pan.

Entrées

The first impression is usually a lasting one

so it's crucial to start any meal with a great entrée. The purpose of an entreé is to tempt the palate and make the tastebuds tingle with anticipation. This section provides some classic and contemporary dishes, which are sure to whet the appetite.

Curried Mussel Soup with Bagel Crisps

I featured this mussel soup in my pop-up restaurant and it received excellent reviews. This velvety textured soup incorporates spices in a subtle way and is a perfect appetiser, warming up the tastebuds.

Serves: 1 / Preparation time: 10 minutes / Cooking time: 10 minutes

½ teaspoon cumin seeds
½ teaspoon coriander seeds
100 g (3½ oz) butter
1 clove garlic, finely chopped
2 eschalots, finely chopped
¼ teaspoon turmeric
50 ml (2 fl oz/¼ cup) mussel stock (see below)
120 ml (4 fl oz/½ cup) coconut milk
½ teaspoon sugar
⅛ teaspoon salt
5 mussels in their shells, cleaned
Oil, for frying
2–3 bagel crisps or sliced baguette

FOR THE MUSSEL STOCK
5 mussels in their shells, cleaned
475 ml (16 fl oz/2 cups) water

To make the stock, place the mussels in a saucepan, add the water, bring to the boil and boil on a medium heat for 10 minutes. Strain and set the liquid aside.

Dry roast the ground cumin and coriander seeds in a small frying pan set over medium heat, then grind to a powder in a mortar and using a pestle.

Add 30 g (1 oz) of the butter to a saucepan and set over medium heat. Sauté the garlic and eschalots in the butter for 1 minute. Add the turmeric, ground cumin and ground coriander and cook for 30 seconds. Add the mussel stock and coconut milk and bring to the boil. Add the sugar and salt and simmer for 1 minute. Strain through a sieve into another pan. Add the rest of the butter and bring to the boil.

Cook the mussels in a hot saucepan with a little oil until they open. Place them in a serving dish and pour the soup on top. Serve with bagel crisps.

Aloo Tikki

'Aloo' means potato and 'tikki' means cutlets or croquets. Aloo tikki is the base ingredient in chaat and a popular Mumbai dish known as ragada patties. This mildly spiced potato patty is perfect as a starter served with sweet and tangy mint chutney.

Serves: 4 / Preparation time: 30 minutes / Cooking time: 20 minutes

500 g (1 lb 2 oz) potatoes, diced
½ teaspoon ground turmeric
1 teaspoon chilli powder
½ teaspoon salt
½ bunch fresh coriander (cilantro), finely chopped
30 g (1 oz/½ cup) breadcrumbs
30 g (1 oz/¼ cup) fine semolina
12 tablespoon oil

FOR THE MINT CHUTNEY
1 cup fresh coriander (cilantro) leaves
1 cup fresh mint leaves
1 green chilli
Juice of 1 lemon
½ teaspoon salt
1 teaspoon sugar

To make the aloo tikki, cook the potatoes in a large pan of boiling water until they are cooked through. Mash well, then stir through the turmeric, chilli powder, salt, chopped coriander and breadcrumbs until the mixture comes together as a dough. Make round patties from the potato mixture and roll in semolina to coat. Heat the oil in a frying pan and fry the potato patties on each side until golden brown.

To make the mint chutney, blend all the ingredients to a fine paste in a blender. Serve with the aloo tikki.

Pani Puri

For me, pani puri creates nostalgic memories. As teenagers, friends would get together and race on our bikes to the local thela (vendor) for pani puri as an evening ritual. Pani puri is the perfect balance of four key elements: sweet, savoury, salty and hot. It makes for an interesting snack.

Serves: 4 / Preparation time: 10 minutes / Cooking time: 30 minutes

1 bunch of mint
2 green whole chillies
5–6 peppercorns
1 teaspoon of amchoor powder
(dried mango powder)
½ teaspoon salt
1 teaspoon sugar
2 teaspoons lime juice

FOR THE STUFFING
1 boiled potato
¼ teaspoon turmeric
¼ teaspoon chilli powder
⅛ teaspoon salt
1 packet puffed puris
2 teaspoons Date and Tamarind
Chutney (see recipe)

To make pani puri water, blend the mint, chillies, peppercorns, amchoor powder in a large bowl and pour on 1 litre (1 ¾ pints) of cold water. Add the salt, sugar and lime juice.

To make the stuffing, lightly mash the potato to a chunky consistency. Add the turmeric, chilli powder and salt and mix well.

Make a hole on one side of a puri and stuff with potato mixture, ½ teaspoon of date and tamarind chutney and 2 tablespoons of pani puri water. Eat immediately before the puri turns soggy.

Grilled Scallops with Mint and Pea Purée and Tomato Relish

Scallops, pea, mint, tomato and chorizo are a classic combination. I have added an Indian twist to this recipe with the tomato relish.

Serves: 1 / Preparation time: 10 minutes / Cooking time: 15 minutes

20 g (¾ oz) butter
55 g (2 oz/½ cup) frozen peas
½ bunch of mint
1 teaspoon sugar
¼ teaspoon salt
3 teaspoons vegetable oil
3 scallops
60 g (2 oz) chorizo
3 teaspoons Spicy Tomato Relish
(see recipe)
3 tablespoons water

FOR THE WATERCRESS SALAD
Juice of 1 lemon
1 teaspoon olive oil
Salt and pepper
½ cup (20 g) watercress leaves

Melt the butter in a saucepan over medium heat, then sauté the peas in the butter for 5 minutes, or until cooked through.

Combine the peas with the mint, sugar and salt in a blender and blend until a fine purée. Set aside.

In a pan, heat 1 teaspoon of oil on high heat and sear the scallops on one side for about 1 minute, or until cooked through.

Meanwhile, in a frying pan, heat the rest of the oil and toss the chorizo through for about 3 minutes, then set aside.

To make vinaigrette for the watercress salad, combine the lemon juice, olive oil, salt and pepper in a small bowl and whisk to mix.

Smear the pea purée on the plate, place 3 scallops on the purée, then add the chorizo. Spoon the spicy tomato relish on the chorizo. Add the watercress to the plate and drizzle vinaigrette over the top.

Chaat

My inspiration for this chaat comes from Northern India and China. It is made in a traditional way but is served like the Chinese dish san choy bau. The iceberg lettuce provides extra crunch and freshness to the dish, which is packed with flavours.

Serves: 4 / Preparation time: 20 minutes / Cooking time: 40 minutes

To make shev or bhujia, mix the besan flour, hot oil, turmeric, salt and water together in a bowl until a tough dough is formed. Use a potato ricer to make noodles out of the dough.

Heat the remaining oil in a deep pan, then deep fry the noodles until golden and crispy, about 3–4 minutes.

Roughly break the aloo tikki and mix with 2 tablespoons of date and tamarind chutney and 2 tablespoon of pani puri water in a bowl. Spoon the aloo tiki mixture into an iceberg lettuce leaf, drizzle yogurt over and scatter 1 teaspoon of mixed onion and tomato on top.

Drizzle with another teaspoon of date and tamarind chutney and garnish with fresh coriander and shev.

4 Aloo Tikkis (see recipe)
½ cup Date and Tamarind Chutney (see recipe)
475 ml (16 fl oz/2 cups) Pani Puri water (see recipe)
4 iceberg lettuce leaves
55 ml (2 fl oz/¼ cup) natural (plain) yogurt
1 onion, chopped
1 tomato, diced
¼ cup fresh coriander (cilantro), chopped

FOR THE SHEV OR BHUJIA
115 g (4 oz/1 cup) besan or chickpea (gram) flour
1 tablespoon oil, heated
½ teaspoon turmeric
½ teaspoon salt
120 ml (4 fl oz/½ cup) water
1 litre (1¾ pints) vegetable oil

Masala Papadum

As a kid, I was always more interested in eating the crunchy papadums than the entrées or main meals when we went to restaurants. When eating out, papadums are usually put on the table as soon as you are seated. It's like the entertainment sidekick; it keeps you busy and happy until the main show begins!
Masala papadums reminds me of nachos, so I have 'nachofied' my papadum. The creamy texture of the avocado complements the crunch.

Serves: 2 / Preparation time: 5 minutes / Cooking time: 5 minutes

Break the papadums into 6–8 pieces so they're a similar size to nacho chips. Cook a few pieces at a time in the microwave in 30-second bursts until golden brown.

Roughly mash the avocado in a mixing bowl. Add the onion, tomato, coriander, lime juice, chat masala, chilli powder and salt and mix together to make guacamole.

Put the guacamole in the centre of a serving plate, arrange the papadums around and sprinkle the cheese on top. Eat as presented, or use a cook's blowtorch to make the Parmesan sizzle until golden brown.

6 papadums
1 avocado, peeled and pitted
½ Spanish (Bermuda) onion, finely diced
1 tomato, diced
¼ cup chopped coriander (cilantro)
Juice of 1 lime
2 teaspoons chat masala
⅛ teaspoon red chilli powder
⅛ teaspoon salt
20 g (¾ oz/¼ cup) Parmesan cheese, grated (shredded)

Kanda Bhaji/Onion Fritters

When it's drizzling outside and there's a chill in the air, there's nothing like hot and crunchy kanda bhaji and a cup of chai to enjoy while you sit back and relax until the rain stops.

Serves: 4 / Preparation time: 10 minutes / Cooking time: 10 minutes

Heat the oil in a deep saucepan. Meanwhile, wash the sliced onion in cold water.

Make the batter by combining the flour, chilli powder, turmeric, salt, bicarbonate of soda and water in a bowl and beating with a whisk until it is lump-free. Add the onion to the batter and stir well to coat.

Deep fry 1 tablespoon of the coated onion mixture at a time for 2 minutes, or until golden brown and crispy. Serve with Spicy Tomato Relish (see recipe).

1 litre (1¾ pints) vegetable oil
1 onion, sliced
90 g (3½ oz/1 cup) chickpea (gram)
  flour
1 teaspoon red chilli powder
1 teaspoon turmeric
1 teaspoon salt
¼ teaspoon bicarbonate of soda
  (baking soda)
250 ml (8 fl oz/1 cup) water
Salt and pepper, to taste
Spicy Tomato Relish (see recipe), to
  serve

Indian Club Sandwich with Mixed Vegetable Chips

The vegetarian club sandwich reminds me of my college days. The crunch of cucumber with soft potato and tangy tomato in the sandwich makes it an ideal afternoon snack.

Serves: 2 / Preparation time: 10 minutes / Cooking time 20 minutes

80 g (3 oz/1 cup) coconut, freshly grated (shredded)
1 bunch fresh coriander (cilantro)
2 teaspoons sugar
½ teaspoon salt
Juice of 1 lemon
1 potato, thinly sliced
55 g (2 oz) butter
6 slices white bread
1 cucumber, thinly sliced
1 tomato, thinly sliced
Leaves from ½ lettuce
1 green chilli
Spicy Tomato Relish (see recipe), to serve

FOR THE CHIPS
1 litre (1¾ pints) vegetable oil
1 parsnip
1 carrot
1 baby beetroot
Salt and pepper, to taste

To make coconut and coriander chutney, in a blender, process the coconut, coriander, sugar, salt and lemon juice until it is a fine purée.

Bring a large pan of water to the boil, add the potato slices and boil for 10 minutes until just tender. Spread butter on the bread slices and coat with the coconut and coriander chutney. Arrange the tomato and cucumber slices on one slice of the bread. Top with a second slice. Arrange the potato and lettuce leaves on top of the second piece of bread and top with another slice of bread. Toast the sandwich, if you like, or eat it as it is. To serve, remove the crust and slice diagonally twice to make 4 triangles.

To make the chips, heat the oil in a saucepan. Meanwhile, thinly slice the parsnip, carrots and baby beetroot and deep fry for 2–3 minutes, or until crispy and golden brown. Dust with salt and pepper.

Serve the sandwich with chips and Spicy Tomato Relish (see recipe).

Oysters with Chorizo, Chilli and Garlic Relish

Summer days and fresh oysters are a perfect combination. Fresh, soft and almost melting in the mouth, these oysters are served with sweet-and-sour chorizo.

Serves: 1 / Preparation time: 10 minutes / Cooking time: 10 minutes

1 tablespoon olive oil
2 garlic cloves, crushed (minced)
2 red chillies, finely chopped
½ Spanish (Bermuda) onion, finely chopped
60 g (2 oz) chorizo, finely chopped
1 tablespoon balsamic vinegar
¼ teaspoon salt
1 tablespoon brown sugar
Rock salt, to serve
3 oysters, shucked
½ teaspoon lime juice
1 teaspoon of micro chervil leaves, to garnish

In a saucepan heat the olive oil, then add the garlic, chilli and onion and sauté for 2 minutes until the onion is translucent. Add the chorizo and sauté for another 2 minutes. Add the balsamic vinegar, salt and sugar, stir and cook for 3–5 minutes on low heat, then set aside.

Place rock salt on a serving plate with three shucked oysters, drizzle lime juice on the oysters and spoon ½ teaspoon of chorizo mixture on top. Garnish with chervil leaves.

Coriander Rolls

If India had the concept of high tea, this dish would be a feature of it. The coconut and coriander provide a burst of freshness while the thin outer layer literally melts in the mouth.

Makes: 20 / Preparation time: 5 minutes / Cooking time: 15 minutes

475 ml (16 fl oz/2 cups) buttermilk
90 g (3½ oz/1 cup) chickpea (gram) flour
1 teaspoon sugar
⅛ teaspoon salt
1 teaspoon turmeric

FILLING
1 cup coriander (cilantro), chopped
1 green chillies, finely chopped
80 g (3 oz/1 cup) freshly grated (shredded) coconut
⅛ teaspoon salt
1 teaspoon sugar
Juice of ½ lemon
3 tablespoons vegetable oil
1 teaspoon of mustard seeds
2 teaspoons Date and Tamarind Chutney (see recipe)

To make the dough, in a saucepan, mix the buttermilk, chickpea flour, sugar, salt and turmeric and cook over medium heat while whisking constantly to avoid and break up any lumps. Keep whisking until the dough comes away from the sides of the saucepan. Test the consistency of the dough by spreading a small amount on a clean baking sheet. Leave to cool, then using your fingertips, try rolling the dough. If it is cooked it will come straight off the baking sheet, otherwise cook the dough a little more.

Once the dough is cooked, divide it between 2 clean baking sheets and spread evenly using a spatula. Leave it to cool completely then make serrations about 3–4 cm (1¼–1¾ in) apart using a knife.

To make the filling, in a bowl, mix the coriander and chillies with the coconut, salt and sugar. Stir in the lemon juice.

In a small pan, heat the oil, and sauté the mustard seeds until they pop. Turn off the heat and set aside until cool.

Drizzle the cooled oil over the two sheets of dough. Drizzle date and tamarind sauce on top. Scatter over the coconut mixture reserving 1 teaspoon for a garnish. Start rolling the roulade from one end, rolling it as tight as possible so the stuffing does not fall out. Garnish with the reserved mixture.

Coconut-rumbed Shrimp with Sweet-and-Sour Sauce Served on a Bed of Apple and Green Mango

The inspiration for this dish comes from the cuisine of Vietnam. I just love that country's use of fresh produce and the balance of flavours they create. Crunchy, spicy shrimp dipped in a sweet-and-sour sauce create a flavour explosion in the mouth.

Serves: 2 / Preparation time: 15 minutes / Cooking time: 15 minutes

To make a sweet-and-sour sauce, mix all the ingredients together in a small bowl and stir until the sugar dissolves.

To make the coconut-crumbed shrimp, heat the oil in a saucepan. Mix the coconut, turmeric, chilli powder and salt together in a small bowl and set aside.

In another bowl, whisk the egg to make an egg wash. Dip the shrimp in the egg wash and then in the coconut mixture until evenly coated. Fry until the shrimp just turn pink, remove from the pan and rest.

On a plate, make a bed of julienned apple and mango. Place the shrimp on top. Serve with the dipping sauce.

120 ml (4 fl oz/½ cup) oil
20 g (¾ oz/¼ cup) coconut, freshly grated (shredded)
½ teaspoon turmeric
½ teaspoon red chilli powder
¼ teaspoon salt
1 egg
4 large shrimp (prawns), cleaned and deveined
1 green apple, finely sliced
1 green mango, finely sliced

FOR THE SWEET-AND-SOUR SAUCE
30 ml rice wine vinegar
2 teaspoons soy sauce
2 teaspoon sugar
1 red chilli, finely chopped
¼ teaspoon fish sauce (nam pla)
1 teaspoon water

Scallop Bhel

This dish is a fusion of fresh seafood with the popular dish bhel. The soft texture of scallops combines well with crispy puffed rice and shev. The date and tamarind chutney adds sweetness, which lifts the flavours of the dish.

Serves: 2 / Preparation time: 10 minutes / Cooking time: 10 minutes

Finely dice the onion and tomato and put both in a small bowl. Mix in the lemon juice, coriander, chilli powder, ground cumin and ground coriander to make a salsa.

In a frying pan heat the oil and sear the scallops on one side over high heat for 1 minute.

Make a bed of shev on each scallop shell, place the scallops on top with 1 teaspoon of the salsa. Drizzle date and tamarind chutney on top and garnish with puffed rice, shev and chopped coriander.

½ Spanish (Bermuda) onion
1 tomato
1 teaspoon lemon juice
2 teaspoon chopped coriander (cilantro)
¼ teaspoon chilli powder
¼ teaspoon ground cumin
½ teaspoon ground coriander
1 teaspoon vegetable oil
4 scallops with roe discarded, but retaining their shells
30 g (1 oz/¼ cup) shev (crispy chickpea noodles)
2 tablespoons Date and Tamarind Chutney (see recipe)
15 g (½ oz/1 cup) puffed rice
Fresh coriander (cilantro), to garnish

Vegetable Garden

This is a fancy version of vegetables and dips, made under the guidance of Heston, and is worth the effort just for the taste. The tangy gribiche with the addition of crunchy capers and gherkins can be used as a dip with crackers or vegetables. Have all the ingredients at room temperature before you begin.

Serves: 2 / Preparation time: 10 minutes / Cooking time: 10 minutes

Cook the Brussels sprouts by boiling or steaming for 5–8 minutes and set aside to cool down.

To make gribiche, put the egg yolks, mustard and vinegar in a mixing bowl. Add salt and pepper. Place the bowl on a damp dish towel to keep it steady, and gradually pour in the oil in a thin stream, whisking all the time with the other hand, until it begins to thicken and forms an emulsion. You could do this in a food processor, if you like. When all the oil has been incorporated and the mayonnaise is thick, stir in the lemon juice and adjust the seasoning to taste. Add the rinsed and chopped capers, chervil, chopped gherkin and Worcestershire sauce and stir through to incorporate.

In a deep dish, add the gribiche to the base; top with dried and chopped black olives. Arrange the vegetables like a garden bed in the gribiche.

2 Brussels sprouts
2 tablespoons dried black olives
  or finely chopped black olives,
  drained on kitchen paper
2 baby radishes
2 baby carrots
2 baby zucchini (courgettes), with
  flowers

FOR THE GRIBICHE
2 hard-boiled egg yolks
1 teaspoon Dijon mustard
1 teaspoon white wine vinegar
Salt
Freshly cracked black pepper
250 ml (8fl oz/1 cup) sunflower or
  canola oil
2 teaspoons lemon juice
1 tablespoon capers, rinsed and
  chopped
1 tablespoon chopped chervil
1 tablespoon chopped gherkin
1 teaspoon Worcestershire sauce

Main meals

This section includes some of my favourite foods. Slow-cooked Kolhapuri goat is my signature dish, while poached salmon is my version of fish curry with rice. There are vegetarian delights too, such as Indian Vegetarian Sliders and Karanataka Risotto as well as my favourite vegetarian dish, Palak Paneer. This section would be incomplete without Butter Quail and Biryani.

Potato Tortillas with Yogurt and Peanut Chutney

As a student in the USA, I occasionally relied on tortillas as a substitue for roti or naan. When I craved potato paratha. I would make it just like this. This recipe is a quick fix for stuffed paratha and retains the traditional paratha flavours.

Serves: 2 / Preparation time: 10 minutes / Cooking time: 30 minutes

2 tortillas
55 g (2 oz/½ cup) Cheddar cheese, grated (shredded)
½ teaspoon of ghee or butter

FOR THE POTATO STUFFING
2 medium potatoes
1 Thai red chilli
1 cm (⅜ in) piece of root ginger
2 garlic cloves
1 tablespoon vegetable oil
¼ teaspoon cumin seeds
¼ teaspoon turmeric
1 medium onion, diced
¼ teaspoon salt
¼ teaspoon sugar
½ teaspoon lime juice
¼ teaspoon ground cumin
¼ teaspoon ground coriander
¼ teaspoon ground cinnamon

To make the potato stuffing, boil the potatoes whole in a large pan of water until cooked through, about 20 minutes. Peel the potatoes and lightly mash them. Set aside.

In a mortar and with a pestle, pound the chilli, ginger and garlic. Meanwhile, in a saucepan, heat the vegetable oil over medium heat and sauté the cumin seeds and turmeric. Add the onion and the chilli, ginger and garlic paste and sauté for 2 minutes, or until the onions are translucent. Add the potatoes, salt, sugar, lime juice, ground cumin, coriander and cinnamon and cook for 1–2 minutes.

FOR THE SALSA
100 g (3½ oz) can sweet corn kernels
1 small tomato, diced
1 teaspoon lime juice
¼ teaspoon salt
1 teaspoon finely chopped coriander
(cilantro) leaves

FOR THE PEANUT AND
YOGURT CHUTNEY
55 g (2 oz/½ cup) roasted peanuts,
crushed
75 g (2½ oz/⅓ cup) natural (plain)
yogurt
2 garlic cloves
1 green chilli
1 teaspoon oil
¼ teaspoon mustard seeds
¼ teaspoon turmeric
¼ teaspoon salt
½ teaspoon sugar
¼ teaspoon lemon juice

To make the salsa, mix all the ingredients together in a small bowl and set aside.

Onto one half of the tortilla spoon 2 tablespoons of the potato mixture and 2 teaspoons of the salsa and spread evenly. Scatter cheese on top and fold the uncoated side of the tortilla over the stuffing to make a half-moon. Lightly coat both sides with ghee or butter. Heat a griddle on a stovetop and place the tortilla on the griddle. Cook on each side for about 1 minute.

To make the peanut chutney, in a bowl, mix the crushed peanuts with the yogurt. Pound the garlic and green chilli in a mortar with a pestle and spoon it on top of the yogurt mixture but do not mix the two.

Meanwhile, in a pan, heat the oil and sauté the mustard seeds until they pop. Add the turmeric and remove from the heat. Pour the hot oil over the garlic and chilli and mix with the yogurt mixture. Add salt, sugar and lemon juice and mix well. Serve the paratha with peanut and yogurt chutney.

Tandoori-spiced Tuna Tataki with Indian Pickled Mushrooms and Garlic and Coriander Mayo

It is uncommon in India to eat raw fish but the sashimi-grade tuna used in this recipe just melts in the mouth. The heat of the tandoori spice mix is offset by the tangy pickled mushrooms and creamy mayo.

Serves: 2 / Preparation time: 10 minutes / Cooking time: 30 minutes

200 g (7 oz) sashimi-grade tuna
4 tablespoon Tandoori Spice Mix (see recipe)
¼ teaspoon crushed black pepper
1 teaspoon olive oil

FOR THE GARLIC AND CORIANDER MAYO
115 g (4 oz/½ cup) mayonnaise
1 tablespoon chopped coriander (cilantro)
1 garlic clove, crushed (minced)
⅛ teaspoon crushed black pepper
⅛ teaspoon salt

FOR THE PICKLED MUSHROOMS
8 fl oz (250 ml/1 cup) vinegar
115 g (4 oz/½ cup) honey
½ teaspoon coriander seeds
½ teaspoon fenugreek seeds
⅛ teaspoon salt
150 g (5 oz) assorted mushrooms, roughly chopped

To make the garlic and coriander mayo, put all the ingredients in a bowl, stir to combine and set aside.

To prepare the pickling mixture for the mushrooms, combine the vinegar, honey, coriander and fenugreek seeds and salt in a small pan and bring to the boil, over medium heat. Place the mushrooms in a bowl, pour the pickling mixture over the top and set aside for 10–15 minutes, or until the mushrooms are soft.

Slice the tuna into long batons and roll in tandoori spice mix to coat evenly on all sides. Place a frying pan over the heat and when hot drizzle 1 teaspoon of olive oil into the pan. Sear the tuna on each side for 30–40 seconds to make sure it is only cooked on the surface and not inside. Slice the batons into squares each 2 cm (¾ in) thick. Slice the tuna into squares, serve on a bed of mushrooms and drizzle mayo on top.

Konkani Masala Clams with Kokum Drink

Tisrya, a Marathi name for clams, are prevalent around the Konkan coast in western India. While the hot tisrya in this dish are packed full of spice, the cold kokum drink offers the perfect complement. Serve with basmati rice.

Serves: 2 / Preparation time: 20 minutes / Cooking time: 30 minutes

To make the kokum drink, pour the coconut milk, water and kokum into a saucepan, bring to the boil over medium heat and boil for 5 minutes, until the colour turns violet. Remove from the heat and take out the kokum.

Blend the green chilli, garlic and coriander into a paste in a blender. Mix the paste with the coconut milk and add the sugar and salt. Stir to dissolve then strain through a fine sieve. Leave to go cold, then refrigerate until ready to serve.

To make the clams, in a saucepan, heat half the oil and sauté the onion for 3–4 minutes, or until it turns golden brown. Add the chopped ginger, garlic and chilli and sauté for 30 seconds. Add the coconut, coriander and cumin seeds, turmeric and kokum, and sauté for another 2 minutes. Remove the kokums, set aside and blend the remaining ingredients in a blender until a fine paste. Sauté the paste with 1 teaspoon of oil until it starts separating.

Meanwhile, in a large pan, heat 1 teaspoon of oil, tip in the clams and heat until they open, 1–2 minutes. Discard any unopened clams. Take the meat out of the opened clams and discard the shells. Add the clam meat to the paste and cook for 30 seconds. Stir in the fresh coriander.

Serve the clam meat in a bowl and the chilled drink in a shot glass.

2 tablespoons vegetable oil
1 onion
2 cm (¾ in) piece of root ginger, peeled and chopped
2 whole garlic cloves
1 finely chopped green chilli
20 g (¾ oz/¼ cup) coconut, freshly grated (shredded)
1 teaspoon coriander seeds
1 teaspoon cumin seeds
½ teaspoon turmeric
10 kokum or mangosteen
500 g (1 lb 2 oz) clams
1 teaspoon coriander (cilantro), finely chopped
Basmati rice, to serve

FOR THE KOKUM DRINK
600 ml (1 pint) coconut milk
250 ml (8 fl oz/1 cup) water
10 kokums or mangosteen
1 green chilli
1 garlic clove
½ cup fresh coriander (cilantro)
2 tablespoons sugar
1 teaspoon salt

Shoukat Chacha's Biryani

Traditionally Biryani is cooked in a clay pot on a coal-fired cooking source and is sealed to makes sure the steam generated by cooking doesn't escape. This recipe uses the same principles but uses modern cooking techniques. The rice is cooked by the juices released from the meat; the taste is spectacular and the meat is tender.

Serves: 6 / Preparation time: 30 minutes / Cooking time: 2 hours 30 minutes

Pour the water into a large pot, add the salt and the rice, bring to the boil and boil for 10–15 minutes. It should only be minimally cooked through at this stage. Remove from the heat, drain all the water and set aside.

Meanwhile, in a saucepan, heat most of the oil and add the cardamoms, peppercorns, cloves, cinnamon and bay leaves and sauté for 1 minute. Preheat the oven to 160°C/325°F/Gas mark 3.

Make a paste of ginger, garlic, mint and green chilli in a blender, add to the saucepan and sauté for 1 minute. Add the onions and cook for 3–4 minutes, or until translucent. Add tomato paste, garam masala and chilli powder and cook for another 1 minute. Add the yogurt and goat or lamb and cook for 5 minutes.

Meanwhile, in a heavy pan, heat 1 teaspoon of oil, then arrange discs of potato on the base. Layer the meat mixture on top of the potato, then the rice and finish with a layer of fried shallots on top.

Heat the ghee and pour it over the rice. Seal the pot with aluminium foil and tightly place the lid on top so that no steam can escape or the rice will not cook. Bake in the oven for 2 hours. Open the lid just before serving and serve with Cucumber Raita (see recipe).

1.75 litres (3 pints/8 cups) water
1 tablespoon salt
600 g (1 lb 6 oz/3 cups) basmati rice

FOR THE BIRYANI
50 ml (2 fl oz/¼ cup) vegetable oil
6 green cardamom pods
3 black cardamom pods
15 black peppercorns
6 cloves
2 cinnamon sticks (quills)
4 bay leaves
5 cm (2 in) piece of root ginger
8 garlic cloves
½ bunch mint
2 green chillies
2 onions, sliced
2 tablespoons tomato paste
2 teaspoons garam masala
2 teaspoons chilli powder
50 ml (2 fl oz/¼ cup) plain (natural) yogurt
600 g (1 lb 6 oz) diced leg or shoulder of goat or lamb
1 potato, peeled and sliced into 2 mm (⅛ in) discs
120 ml (4 fl oz/½ cup) shallots, fried
50 ml (2 fl oz/¼ cup) ghee or clarified butter
Cucumber Raita (see recipe), to serve

Urid and Mung Fritters with Sweet-and-Sour Yogurt

Urid legume fritters originate from Southern India but are now common across the country. These crispy fritters served with chilled sweet-and-sour yogurt, and topped with tangy date and tamarind chutney are a perfect dinner for hot summer's night.

Serves: 8 / Preparation time: 4 hours / Cooking time: 20 minutes

Rinse and soak the urid and mung dals separately in warm water and set aside for at least 3–4 hours. Remove some of the excess water from the dals, then blend each separately with two chillies into a purée. Mix the batters together with the salt and bicarbonate of soda.

To make the sweet-and-sour yogurt, mix the yogurt, salt and sugar together in a bowl until the sugar dissolves.

In a small frying pan, heat 1 tablespoon of oil and sauté the mustard seeds, curry leaves and red chillies until the mustard seeds pop. Turn the heat off and mix the oil with the yogurt, leave to cool then refrigerate until needed.

Meanwhile, to make the fritters, heat the oil in a large frying pan over medium heat, and deep fry the batter 1 tablespoon at a time for 5–7 minutes, or until golden brown and crispy. Drizzle Date and Tamarind Chutney on top and dust with red chilli powder. Serve with yogurt.

350 g (12 oz/1½ cups) urid dal
115 g (4 oz/½ cup) mung dal
4 green chillies
2 teaspoons salt
½ teaspoon of bicarbonate soda (baking soda)
½ litre (17 fl oz/2 cups) oil, for deep frying
2 teaspoon of Date and Tamarind Chutney (see recipe), to serve
¼ teaspoon chilli powder, to serve
Plain (natural) yogurt, to serve

FOR THE SWEET-AND-SOUR YOGURT
1 litre (1¾ pints) plain (natural) yogurt
1 teaspoon salt
5 teaspoons sugar
1 tablespoon oil
1 teaspoon mustard seeds
Handful of curry leaves
3 dry red chillies

Palak Paneer with Indian Pickled Baby Vegetables and Baguette Crisps

Palak paneer is a thick curry sauce loved all around the world. I learned how to make fresh paneer from a restaurateur in Mumbai a few years ago and always make it at home. However, most Indian grocery stores now make fresh paneer available, which tastes as good as homemade. This dish contains plenty of different tastes and textures. Soft paneer with spicy sauce, tangy pickle and crunchy crisps makes it a delight to eat. This is a meal in one as it has rice, bread, paneer and pickle.

Serves: 2 / Preparation time: 20 minutes / Cooking time: 60 minutes

1 litre (1¾ pints) whole milk
1 teaspoon salt
Juice of 2 lemons
2 tablespoons cooked saffron rice
1 egg
15 g (½ oz/¼ cup) breadcrumbs
⅛ teaspoon salt
Vegetable oil, for frying

FOR THE SPINACH SAUCE
1 bunch spinach
1 teaspoon vegetable oil
½ teaspoon mustard seeds
½ teaspoon turmeric
2 cm (¾ in) piece of root ginger
2 garlic cloves, finely chopped
1 medium onion, diced
1 tomato, diced
1 teaspoon ground cumin
1 teaspoon ground coriander
½ teaspoon chilli powder
½ teaspoon garam masala
⅛ teaspoon salt
1 teaspoon sugar
120 ml (4 fl oz) ½ cup thickened
(double or heavy) cream

Heat the milk in a saucepan with the salt until it is 77°C/170°F. Stir in the lemon juice and once the milk splits, cook until the temperature reaches 81°C/178°F. Remove from the heat and strain into a bowl through a fine sieve lined with muslin. The paneer, or fats, will be retained in the sieve. Mix the paneer, cooked rice, egg, breadcrumbs and salt in a bowl until well combined. Shape the paneer mixture, a spoonful at a time into small discs about 2 cm (¾ in) thick and refrigerate for 1 hour, or until firm.

Meanwhile, to make the spinach sauce, bring a saucepan of water to the boil, then add the spinach. Cook for 5 minutes, or until the leaves wilt. Transfer to a bowl of cold water for 2 minutes. Drain and set the spinach aside.

In a saucepan, heat 1 teaspoon of vegetable oil and sauté the mustard seeds until they pop. Add the turmeric, ginger, garlic and onion and sauté until the onion is translucent. Add the diced tomato, ground cumin, coriander, chilli powder and garam masala and sauté for another 20 seconds. Add the blanched spinach, salt, sugar and cream and cook for 8–10 minutes on medium heat, or until the sauce thickens. Blend the sauce into a purée and pass it through a fine sieve. Pour into a piping bag or squeeze bottle and stand in warm water.

FOR THE PICKLE

2 baby carrots, peeled and finely
sliced
2 baby turnips, peeled and
finely sliced
2 baby radishes, sliced
120 ml (4 fl oz) ½ cup white vinegar
1 teaspoon coriander seeds
50 ml (2 fl oz/¼ cup) honey

FOR THE BAGUETTE CRISPS

1 baguette
Butter, to brush
Vegetable oil, for frying

To make the pickle, put the sliced carrots, turnip and radishes in a large bowl. Heat the vinegar, coriander seeds and honey in a small pan, then pour the pickling mixture over the vegetables and set aside for 15 minutes.

For the baguette crisps, preheat the oven to 180°C/350°F/ Gas mark 4. Thinly slice the baguette and brush butter on the discs. Bake for 5 minutes until golden brown.

Remove the paneer from the refrigerator. Coat the base of a frying pan with vegetable oil and sear the discs for 1 minute on each side until golden brown.

Arrange the baguette crisps on a plate, top with a paneer disc, pipe spinach sauce on top, then place pickled vegetables on top.

Pan-Fried Rabbit Loin with Parsnip Purée and Pickled Vegetables

Rabbit is very easy to cook and absolutely delicious. Root vegetables complement it very well. Rabbit and Indian flavours go hand in hand so don't be afraid to try rabbit in curries. The dish is sweet with the flavour of parsnips ,which is balanced by the tangy juice of unripened grapes.

Serves: 1 / Preparation time: 20 minutes / Cooking time: 30 minutes

120 ml (4 fl oz/½ cup) white wine

2 tablespoons verjuice

2 tablespoons white wine vinegar

1 teaspoon coriander seeds

1 baby beetroot (beet), thinly sliced into discs

1 baby golden beetroot (beet), thinly sliced into discs

FOR THE SAUCE

1 tablespoon olive oil

2 garlic cloves, roughly chopped

1 small onion, chopped

3 thyme sprigs

¼ bunch chives

2 rabbit legs whole

230 ml (8 fl oz/1 cup) white wine

110 ml (3¾ fl oz) verjuice

2 baby turnips, quartered

30 g (1 oz) butter

To make the pickled vegetables, put the wine, 2 tablespoons of verjuice, the white wine vinegar and coriander seeds in a small saucepan set over medium heat. Bring to the boil, then reduce the heat to a simmer. Cook for 1 minute to allow the alcohol to evaporate. Pour into two bowls then add red beetroot slices to one and golden beetroot slices to the other. Set aside for 30 minutes to pickle, then strain through a sieve. Lightly pat dry with kitchen paper and set aside.

Meanwhile, to make the sauce, put the olive oil in a saucepan set over medium heat. Add the garlic and onion, and cook for 2–3 minutes, or until translucent. Add the leaves from 2 sprigs of thyme, the chives and rabbit legs, and cook for 4–5 minutes, or until caramelised. Add the wine and verjuice, cover with a lid, and cook for 10 minutes. Add the turnip quarters to the pan, and continue to cook for about 20 minutes, or until the stock is thickened and the turnips are cooked through. Remove the turnips and set aside. Discard the rabbit legs.

Strain the stock into a clean bowl and slowly whisk in the butter until the sauce is thick and glossy. Set aside.

To make a purée, place the turnips in a small saucepan, cover with

FOR THE PURÉE
2 baby turnips, peeled and roughly
chopped
20 g (¾ oz) goat's cheese
1 tablespoon oil
Salt and pepper
2 rabbit loins
1 baby carrot, peeled and sliced into
ribbons
1 baby purple carrot, peeled and
sliced into ribbons

water, set over medium heat and bring to the boil. Simmer for about 15 minutes, or until soft. Transfer the cooked turnips to a blender, add half the goat's cheese and blend to a paste. Push the paste through a fine sieve into a clean bowl, season to taste with salt and pepper, and set aside.

Heat the remaining tablespoon of oil in a frying pan set over medium-high heat. Season the rabbit loins, and fry for about 1–2 minutes on each side, or until caramelised. Remove from the pan and allow to rest for 2 minutes before slicing.

To serve, spoon purée onto the plates, top with rabbit slices, pickled vegetables, carrot ribbons and the rest of the goat's cheese. Drizzle with sauce, garnish with thyme sprigs and season to taste.

Spicy Beef Roast and Red Wine Jus

In India cow is considered holy so beef is rarely available. For those who prefer not to eat beef, replace it with lamb in this recipe. This dish is complemented perfectly with a dollop of Green Mango Chutney and Naan Bread.

Serves: 4 / Preparation time: 20 minutes / Cooking time: 60 minutes

8 garlic cloves
3 cm (1¼ in) piece of root ginger
½ teaspoon red chilli powder
¼ teaspoon turmeric
½ teaspoon garam masala
¼ teaspoon salt
Juice of ½ lime
1 tablespoon olive oil
1 kg (2¼ lb) Scotch fillet (rib eye)
1 tablespoon Green Mango Chutney
(see recipe), to serve
1 Naan Bread (see recipe), to serve

FOR THE RED WINE JUS
1 teaspoon olive oil
1 shallot, finely chopped
50 ml (2 fl oz/¼ cup) red wine
15 g (½ oz) butter
½ teaspoon sugar
⅛ teaspoon salt

To make spice paste, finely blend 5 cloves of garlic, the ginger, red chilli powder, turmeric, garam masala, salt and lime juice with 1 teaspoon of water using a pestle and mortar.

Heat the olive oil in a roasting pan until it smokes. Place the Scotch fillet and remaining garlic cloves in the pan and brown the meat on both sides. Apply the spice paste to the meat and place the roasting pan in the oven for 30 minutes until the internal temperature of the meat reaches 52°C/126°F. Remove from the oven and wrap with aluminium foil. Set aside to rest for 10–15 minutes. Slice thinly and arrange on a plate.

To make the jus, heat the oil in a frying pan set over medium heat. Add the shallots and cook for 1 minute. Add the red wine and reduce until thick and glossy. Strain, discard the shallots and transfer the liquid to a small pan. Place the pan on medium heat, add the butter, sugar and salt and whisk until the butter is melted.

Arrange sliced beef on the plate. Drizzle jus on top and serve with green mango chutney and naan bread.

Buttered Quail

Quail has a distinct and strong flavour and requires a sauce that complements the game-like flavour of the meat but doesn't overpower it. Measure carefully the quantity of spices used in this dish. Serve with buttered Naan Bread to scoop up the sauce.

Serves: 1 / Preparation time: 30 minutes / Cooking time: 30 minutes

Heat a frying pan over medium heat, add the cumin and coriander seeds and dry fry for 1–2 minutes, or until fragrant. Crush in a mortar using a pestle. Set aside.

Make a paste by crushing 4 of the garlic cloves, the ginger, lemon juice, and half of the crushed cumin and coriander seeds in a blender.

Rub 1 tablespoon of the paste onto the quail, place in a ceramic bowl and refrigerate for 30 minutes to marinate.

Meanwhile, melt half the butter in a small pan over medium heat. Add the remaining paste and cook for about 1 minute, or until fragrant. Add the onions and remaining garlic cloves and cook for about 5 minutes, or until translucent. Add the tomatoes and honey, and cook for 5 minutes, or until they start to break down. Transfer to a blender with the remaining cumin and coriander, cloves, cinnamon, nutmeg, cayenne, chilli powder and turmeric, and blend to a purée. Preheat the oven to 180°C/350°F/Gas mark 4.

Melt 50 g (1¾ oz) of the butter in a pan over medium heat. Add the purée and simmer for about 5 minutes, until thickened. Strain through a fine sieve into a clean pan and place over medium heat. Slowly stir in 50 g (1¾ oz) of the butter and all the cream and cook for 5 minutes, stirring regularly. Season with salt. If the sauce separates, whisk in 1–2 tablespoons water until combined.

Place a chargrill pan over high heat. Drizzle the quail with oil. Cook for about 1–2 minutes on each side. Transfer to the oven and bake for 3–5 minutes. Cover loosely with foil, and set aside to rest for 5 minutes. To serve, spoon the sauce onto the plates, top with quail and serve with naan bread spread with the remaining butter.

3 teaspoons cumin seeds
3 teaspoons coriander seeds
6 garlic cloves, sliced
1 cm (⅜ in) piece of root ginger
Juice of 1 lemon
2 quails, deboned
250 g (9 oz) butter
1 large or 2 small onions, finely chopped
2 tomatoes, diced
1 tablespoon honey
¼ teaspoon ground cloves
¼ teaspoon ground cinnamon
¼ teaspoon ground nutmeg
1 teaspoon ground cayenne pepper
1 teaspoon chilli powder
1 teaspoon turmeric
50 ml (2 fl oz/¼ cup) thickened (double, heavy) cream
¼ teaspoon salt
Vegetable oil, to drizzle
Naan Bread (ses recipe), to serve

Coconut Milk Poached Salmon with Spiced Velouté and Caramelised Onion Purée

This is by far one of the more adventurous dishes I have attempted during my pop-up restaurants. The texture of the salmon is unique because it is cooked at low temperature and the velvety and subtle velouté is well balanced with the spicy caramelised onion purée.

Serves: 2 / Preparation time: 20 minutes / Cooking time: 1 hour

Heat 1 tablespoon of oil in a small saucepan and fry the mustard seeds, cumin seeds and curry leaves until the mustard seeds pop, then turn off the heat. Set aside.

In a large saucepan, pour in the coconut milk, then add the cinnamon, cardamom, peppercorns, fenugreek seeds, cloves and coriander seeds. Add the mustard and cumin-infused oil and lower in the salmon fillet. Make sure the salmon is completely submerged. Poach on the stovetop making sure the temperature of the fish is maintained at 43°C/109°F for 1 hour. Scoop the salmon out, retain the cooking liquid and discard the skin. Gently flake the flesh and set aside.

Meanwhile, to make the caramelised onion purée, in a saucepan, heat the oil and add the mustard seeds and curry leaves and let them pop. Add the ginger and garlic and sauté for 20 seconds. Add the onion and turmeric and sauté for 3 minutes, or until the onion is translucent. Then add the tomato paste, chilli powder, ground cumin and ground coriander and sauté for another 1 minute. Add the coconut milk, sugar and salt and cook until the mixture reduces. Using a blender, make into a purée and pass through a sieve into a bowl. Set aside.

1 tablespoon oil
¼ teaspoon mustard seeds
¼ teaspoon ground cumin seeds
6–7 curry leaves
400 ml (14 fl oz/1⅔ cups) coconut milk
1 cinnamon quill (stick)
4 green cardamom pods
10 black peppercorns
¼ teaspoon fenugreek seeds
5 cloves
¼ teaspoon coriander seeds
1 x 200 g (7 oz) salmon fillet, skin on

FOR THE CARAMELISED ONION PURÉE
2 tablespoons vegetable oil
½ teaspoon mustard seeds
5–6 curry leaves
1 cm (⅜ in) root ginger, finely chopped
3–4 garlic cloves, finely chopped
1 medium onion, finely chopped
¼ teaspoon turmeric
1 tablespoon tomato paste
½ teaspoon red chilli powder
1 teaspoon ground cumin
1 teaspoon ground coriander
2 tablespoons coconut milk
1 teaspoon sugar
¼ teaspoon salt

To make the velouté, heat the butter in a saucepan and sauté the chopped shallots for 1 minute. Add the turmeric, ground cumin and ground coriander and the remaining cooking liquid from the salmon. Bring to the boil, season with salt and pour in the cornflour mixture. Once the sauce thickens, turn the heat off and strain through a sieve into a sauce boat.

In a saucepan, heat the vegetable oil until smoking and deep fry the wild rice for 30 seconds or until puffed up. Remove from the oil and drain on kitchen paper.

Place the flaked salmon in a deep dish, pour the velouté around the salmon and add a dollop of caramelised onion purée on top. Garnish with puffed wild rice, placing it on top of the purée.

FOR THE COCONUT VELOUTÉ
10 g (⅓ oz) butter
1 shallot, finely chopped
¼ teaspoon turmeric
¼ teaspoon ground cumin
¼ teaspoon ground coriander
Cooking liquid from the salmon
1 teaspoon vegetable oil
¼ teaspoon salt
5 g cornflour (corn starch) dissolved in 60 ml (2 fl oz/¼ cup) water

FOR THE PUFFED RICE
1 teaspoon wild rice
600 ml (16 fl oz/2 cups) vegetable oil, for deep frying

Pan-Seared Crispy Skin Duck Breast with Shahi Lentils and Fennel Chips

Duck and lentils are a classic French combination. Traditionally sweet sauces complement duck really well so the sweet shahi lentils in this dish work fantastically with duck. The fennel chips complement the aniseed in the lentils and provide crunch.

Serves: 2 / Preparation time: 15 minutes / Cooking time: 30 minutes

Melt the butter in a pan over medium heat. Add the panchphoron, crushed garlic, ginger and red chillies and sauté for 30 seconds. Add the onion and sauté for another 2 minutes. Add the crushed tomatoes and cook for 5 minutes. Add the red chilli powder, coriander, garam masala and cinnamon and cook for 2 minutes. Add the black lentils and simmer on medium heat for 15 minutes. Add the cream, sugar and a pinch of salt and simmer on low heat for another 10 minutes.

Serrate the skin of the duck breasts about 1 cm (3/8 in) apart and rub some salt on the skin. Place skin side down in a cold pan. Heat the pan over medium heat and cook for 10 minutes until the skin becomes crispy and golden brown. Keep removing the excess fat from the pan while the duck is cooking. Turn the duck over and cook for 8 minutes, or until the duck is cooked to medium and is pink inside. Set aside to rest on a wire rack. Slice at an angle.

Thinly slice some fennel chips. To make a smooth batter put the plain flour and salt in a bowl, add some water and beat until lump-free. Dip the chips in the batter and deep fry for 2–3 minutes, or until golden brown.

Serve the duck on a bed of lentils and place the fennel chips on the side.

1 tablespoon butter
1 teaspoon panchphoron
4 garlic cloves, crushed
1.5 cm (½ in) piece root ginger, grated (shredded)
2 red chillies
1 onion, finely chopped
150 g (5 oz) canned crushed tomato
1 teaspoon red chilli powder
1 teaspoon ground coriander
1 teaspoon garam masala
1 cinnamon quill (stick)
300 g (11 oz) canned black lentils
250 ml (8 fl oz/1 cup) single (light) cream
1 teaspoon sugar
Salt and pepper
2 duck breasts, skin on
1 fennel
1 litre (1¾ pints) vegetable oil, for deep frying

FOR THE BATTER
100 g (3½ oz) plain (all-purpose) flour
¼ teaspoon salt
250 ml (8 fl oz) cold water

Indian Vegetarian Sliders with Peanut Chutney and Okra Chips

Vada paav, is a popular spicy vegetarian fast-food dish native to the Indian state of Maharashtra. It consists of a potato fritter sandwiched between two slices of bread. It is also known as an Indian burger. I've reinvented it here. Serve this with Peanut Chutney and Date and Tamarind Chutney.

Serves: 3 / Preparation time: 40 minutes / Cooking time: 20 minutes

4 potatoes
2 cm (¾ in) piece of root ginger, chopped
2 garlic cloves, chopped
2 green chillies, chopped
1 cup coriander (cilantro) leaves, finely chopped
1 teaspoon turmeric
1 teaspoon salt
1 teaspoon cumin seeds
1 teaspoon coriander seeds
30 g (1 oz/½ cup) breadcrumbs
1 litre (1¾ pints) vegetable oil, for deep frying
1 teaspoon Peanut Chutney (see recipe), to serve
1 tablespoon Date and Tamarind Chutney (see recipe), to serve

FOR THE BRIOCHE
250 ml (8 fl oz/1 cup) milk
2 tablespoon butter, melted, plus extra for brushing
1 large egg
425 g (15 oz/3¼ cups) plain (all-purpose) flour, plus extra for dusting
3 tablespoons sugar

To make the brioche, in a bowl, whisk together the milk, melted butter and egg. Pour the milk mixture, flour, sugar, salt and yeast into the bowl of a food processor fitted with a dough hook, and mix for 5 minutes or until a smooth dough is formed. Tip the dough out onto a lightly floured surface and flatten slightly. Using a round 5 cm/2 in cookie cutter, stamp out rounds. Arrange on a lightly greased baking sheet about 5 cm (2 in) apart. Cover with a clean kitchen towel and leave to rise until doubled in size, about 30 minutes.

Meanwhile, boil the potatoes whole in a large pan of boiling water until tender. Remove the skin and mash until smooth. (Don't use a food processor.)

Preheat the oven to 180°C/350°/Gas mark 4.

Make a coarse paste of ginger, garlic and chilli in a mortar and using a pestle. Mix the potatoes with the ginger-garlic paste in a bowl. Add the coriander leaves, turmeric, salt, cumin seeds, coriander seeds and breadcrumbs and stir until well combined. Form the mixture into medium-sized patties. Set aside.

Bake the brioche for 15–18 minutes, or until nicely browned. Brush the tops with a little melted butter while they're hot. Leave to cool on a wire rack.

1 teaspoon salt
2½ teaspoons dry yeast
1 teaspoon butter, melted, for
drizzling

FOR THE BATTER
115 g (4 oz/1 cup) besan or chickpea
(gram) flour
1 teaspoon red chilli powder
1 teaspoon turmeric
¼ teaspoon bicarbonate of soda
(baking soda)
1 teaspoon salt
125 ml (4 fl oz/½ cup) water

FOR THE OKRA CHIPS
100 g (3 ½ oz) okra
⅛ teaspoon salt

To make a thick batter, combine the chickpea flour, chilli powder, turmeric, bicarbonate of soda, salt and water in a large bowl. Whisk until smooth and let it stand.

Heat the oil for deep frying in a deep pan at 180°C/350°F. Dip the potato patties in the batter to coat them evenly, then gently add to the pan of oil and deep fry for 5–7 minutes, or until golden brown.

Thinly slice the okra and fry it in the same oil for 1 minute. Sprinkle with salt.

To assemble the sliders coat the base of each bun with Peanut Chutney, add a potato fritter and drizzle over Date and Tamarind Chutney. Top with the other half of the brioche bun. Secure with a skewer and serve with the okra chips.

Pork Vindaloo Kati Kebab with Green Mango Chutney

Vindaloo originates from Goa on the western coast of India. It was once a Portuguese colony, so there is a strong Portuguese influence on the food. Over time the cuisine of the region has evolved, taking on Indian flavours. Kati Kebab originates from Calcutta or Kolkata on the eastern coastline, so this dish is East meets West Indian style.

Serves: 4 / Preparation time: 20 minutes / Cooking time: 1 hour

250 g (9 oz) pork belly
2 teaspoon rock salt
1 tablespoon vegetable oil
1 onion, diced
¼ teaspoon fenugreek seeds
475 ml (16 fl oz/2 cups) chicken stock
2 eggs
4 tortillas
50 g (2 oz/½ cup) carrots, julienned
½ cup fresh coriander (cilantro), finely chopped
Green Mango Chutney (see recipe), to serve

FOR THE VINDALOO PASTE
3 garlic cloves
2 cm (¾ in) piece root ginger
1 teaspoon cumin seeds, ground
1 teaspoon coriander seeds, ground
1 teaspoon garam masala
2 red chillies
2 tablespoons white vinegar
1 teaspoon sugar
½ teaspoon turmeric

Preheat the oven to 230°C/450°F/Gas mark 8.

Make the vindaloo paste by blending the garlic, ginger, cumin and coriander seeds, garam masala, red chillies, vinegar, sugar and turmeric in a blender.

Take the skin off the pork belly and score with a sharp knife diagonally. Rub in the salt and roast for 20 minutes. Reduce the oven temperature to 200°C/400°F/Gas mark 6 and continue to roast the skin for 1 hour or until it is crispy all over. Break the crispy crackling into small pieces.

Meanwhile, finely slice the pork meat. Heat the oil over medium heat and sauté the onion for 2 minutes, or until translucent. Add the fenugreek seeds and the vindaloo paste and sauté for 30 seconds, then add the pork meat. Cook for 1 minute, add the stock and cook for 20–25 minutes, or until the pork is tender and the sauce thickens.

Beat the eggs in a small bowl. In a non-stick pan, swirl quarter of the egg and place 1 tortilla on the egg before the egg sets. Cook until the egg is golden brown and then remove from the pan, spoon in some of the pork vindaloo mixture, crackling, carrot and coriander and make into roll keeping the egg side outside. Serve with Green Mango Chutney.

Chilli Garlic Crab Served with Fresh Mango, Mooli and Rocket Salad

There is no greater satisfaction than shredding crab meat, sucking every last bit from the shell, then licking chilli and garlic marinade from your fingers. The tastiest meat is in the claws.

Serves: 2 / Preparation time: 15 minutes / Cooking time: 20 minutes

2 blue swimmer crabs or local hard shell crabs
2 tablespoons vegetable oil
Green part of 1 spring onion (scallion), chopped

FOR THE CHILLI PASTE
1 medium onion
2 Thai red chillies
1 long red chilli
5 garlic cloves
3 cm (1¼ in) piece of root ginger, chopped
1 bunch fresh coriander (cilantro) stalks, washed
Juice of 1 lemon
50 ml (2 fl oz/¼ cup) vegetable oil
2 teaspoons sugar
¼ teaspoons salt

FOR THE SALAD
1 ripe mango
1 mooli or daikon
30 g (1 oz) rocket (arugula)
⅛ teaspoon salt
½ teaspoon lemon juice

To make the chilli paste, coarsely chop the onion and add to a blender with both the chillies, garlic, ginger, coriander stalks and lemon juice to a fine paste. In a saucepan, heat the oil and sauté the chilli paste, sugar and salt and let it simmer on low heat for 15 minutes, or until fragrant and the oil starts to separate.

Remove the top shell of the crab and clean it, then quarter the crabs using a sharp knife, or ask your fishmonger to do it for you. In a wok, heat the oil until smoking and add the crab meat. Cook until translucent, 4–5 minutes, then add all the chilli paste and cook for 3–4 minutes. Add in the chopped spring onion and mix through.

To make the salad, dice the mango and julienne the mooli. Toss together with the rocket, salt and ½ teaspoon of lemon juice. Serve salad with the crab.

Lamb Cutlets with Smoked Eggplant Purée, Eggplant Chips and Pickled Baby Vegetables

Known as baingan bharta, smoked eggplant purée is an Indian version of baba ghanoush. The smoky flavour of the eggplant infused with spices complements the crunchy-on-the-outside and tender-on-the-inside texture of the lamb very well.

Serves: 2 / Preparation time: 10 minutes / Cooking time: 30 minutes

For the chips, peel 4–5 thin slices off the eggplant thinly using a vegetable peeler and set aside.

For the purée, using a fork, prick the rest of the eggplant randomly, rub 1 teaspoon of oil on the eggplant and roast over a medium flame until the skin is charred. Alternatively roast it on a barbecue or in the oven at 180°C/350°F/Gas mark 4. Once cooled, remove and discard the skin and coarsely chop the cooked flesh.

In a saucepan, heat the rest of the oil and sauté the mustard seeds until they pop. Add the turmeric, green chilli and garlic and sauté for 30 seconds. Add the onion and cook for 3–5 minutes, or until translucent. Add the tomato and cook for another 2 minutes. Add the curry powder, cumin and coriander, yogurt, eggplant flesh, sugar and 1 teaspoon salt and cook for 4–5 minutes. Tip into a blender with the lime juice and purée until smooth. Set aside.

Meanwhile, in a frying pan, add the oil and fry the eggplant for 2 minutes on each side or until crispy and golden brown. Sprinkle with salt and set aside.

1 eggplant (aubergine)
1 tablespoon vegetable oil
½ teaspoon mustard seeds
½ teaspoon turmeric
1 green chilli, finely chopped
2 garlic cloves, chopped
1 onion, finely chopped
1 tomato, diced
1 tablespoon curry powder
½ teaspoon ground cumin
½ teaspoon ground coriander
2 tablespoons yogurt
1 tablespoon sugar
Salt and pepper
Juice of ½ lime
2 tablespoons vegetable oil, for shallow frying the chips

Preheat the oven to 180°C/350°F/Gas mark 4.

Mix together the breadcrumbs, chilli powder, turmeric and a pinch of salt. Season the lamb cutlets with salt and pepper and sear them in a hot pan with little oil on both sides for 1 minute. Whisk the egg to make the egg wash, dip the lamb cutlets in the egg wash to coat evenly and roll them in the breadcrumb mixture to coat thoroughly. Line a baking sheet with baking paper and arrange the lamb cutlets on top. Bake for 5–7 minutes.

To make the pickled vegetables, slice the radish and parsnips into thin rounds using a mandolin and place in separate bowls. Thinly peel strips of carrots and place in another bowl. In a saucepan, add the honey, vinegar, coriander and mustard seeds and bring to the boil over medium heat. Divide the vinegar mixture between the three bowls of vegetables and leave to soak for 5–10 minutes. Take the vegetables out of the pickling mixture. Serve the lamb cutlets on a bed of eggplant purée, with pickles and chips on the side.

FOR THE BREADCRUMB MIXTURE
30 g (1 oz/½ cup) breadcrumbs
½ teaspoon chilli powder
½ teaspoon turmeric
Salt and pepper
4 lamb cutlets
1 tablespoon oil
1 egg, for the egg wash

FOR THE PICKLED BABY VEGETABLES
1 baby radish
1 baby parsnip
1 baby carrot
1 tablespoon honey
2 tablespoons vinegar
½ teaspoon coriander seeds
½ teaspoon white mustard seeds

Pan-Seared Beef-Eye Fillet Served with Methi Mutter Malai Sauce and Chat Potatoes

Methi or fenugreek can be used as herb, spice or a vegetable. It has a unique bitter taste, which requires balancing with sugar. The chat potatoes coated in dried mango powder are tangy, tasty and crunchy.

Serves: 1 / Preparation time 20 minutes / Cooking time: 60 minutes

To make the methi mutter malai, in a blender make a paste using the ginger, garlic, cashew nuts and green chillies with a little water. In a saucepan, over medium heat, heat the oil, sauté the mustard seeds and turmeric until the mustard seeds pop. Add the onion and sauté for 3–5 minutes, or until translucent. Add the cashew nut paste and sauté for another 2 minutes. Add the fenugreek leaves and peas and cook for 3–4 minutes on medium heat, or until the leaves wilt. Add the sugar and salt and cook for another 1 minute. Turn the heat off and leave to cool. Tip into a blender and process to a smooth purée.

Meanwhile, to cook the meat, in a frying pan, heat 1 teaspoon of oil. Season the beef fillet on both sides and place it in the hot pan. Turn the meat every 15 seconds and cook until medium or as desired. As a guide, cook a 2 cm (¾in) thick piece of steak for 2–3 minutes on each side for rare, 4 minutes on each side for medium, and 5–6 minutes on each side for well-done.

Remove the fillet from the heat and set aside to rest on a plate. In the same pan, make the jus. Add the brandy and flambé it by setting the brandy on fire. Add the beef stock and sugar and reduce until thick. Add the butter to the sauce, stir and heat until dissolved.

To make the chat potatoes, preheat the oven to 180°C/350°F/ Gas mark 4. In a bowl, mix the olive oil, chat masala, salt and the diced potato. Bake in a baking dish for at least 40 minutes or until the potatoes are golden brown.

Serve the beef on a bed of chat potatoes with methi mutter malai on the side.

1 teaspoon oil
1 x 200 g (7 oz) beef eye fillet
   (tenderloin)
Salt and pepper

FOR THE METHI MUTTER MALAI
2 cm (¾ in) piece of root ginger
3 garlic cloves
45 g (1½ oz/⅓ cup) cashew nuts
2 green chillies
1 tablespoon vegetable oil
½ teaspoon mustard seeds
½ teaspoon turmeric
1 medium onion, chopped
1 bunch of fresh fenugreek leaves
   or 1 packet of frozen
55 g (2 oz/½ cup) peas
2 teaspoon sugar

FOR THE JUS
120 ml (4 fl oz/½ cup) brandy
120 ml (4 fl oz/½ cup) beef stock
2 teaspoons sugar
30 g (1 oz) butter

FOR THE CHAT POTATOES
½ teaspoon olive oil
1 tablespoon chat masala
1 large potato, diced

Tri-colour Chicken Kebabs

The three colours of the Indian flag, orange, white and green, are embodied in this dish: chicken with tandoori marinade is orange, reshmi marinade is white and mint marinade is green. Together they present a combination of spicy, creamy and tangy flavours. Serve with couscous for a main meal or serve kebabs as starters.

Serves: 4 / Preparation time: 2 hours / Cooking time: 20 minutes

Soak some wooden skewers in water for at least 2 hours.

To make the tandoori kebab, in a blender, make a smooth paste of the ginger, garlic, tandoori spice powder and lemon juice. Season with salt. Mix the paste with yogurt and brush over one-third of the diced chicken thigh. Let it marinate in a non-metallic dish for at least 2 hours, or overnight.

To make the green kebab, in a blender, make a paste of the ginger, garlic, coriander, mint, green chillies and lemon juice. Season, mix the paste with yogurt and brush over one-third of the chicken and leave to marinate as before.

To make the reshmi kebab, in a blender, make a paste of the ginger, garlic, cashews, green chillies and lemon juice. Season with salt. Mix the paste with the cream and brush over the remaining chicken and leave to marinate as before.

FOR THE TANDOORI KEBAB

2 cm (¾ oz) piece of root ginger

3 garlic cloves

2 tablespoon tandoori spice powder

Juice of 1 lemon

Salt

1 tablespoon natural (plain) yogurt

1 boneless chicken thigh, diced

FOR THE GREEN KEBAB

2 cm (¾ in) piece of root ginger

3 garlic cloves

¼ cup of fresh coriander (cilantro)

¼ cup of fresh mint

2 green chillies

Juice of 1 lemon

Salt

1 tablespoon of plain (natural) yogurt

1 boneless chicken thigh, diced

FOR THE RESHMI KEBAB

2 cm (¾ in) piece of root ginger

3 garlic cloves

30 g (1 oz) cashew nuts

2 green chillies

Juice of 1 lemon

1 tablespoon single (light) cream

1 boneless chicken thigh, diced

To make the couscous, heat the water in a saucepan with the oil and salt. Bring to the boil, turn off the heat and add the couscous. Cover and set aside until ready to serve.

Meanwhile, dice the capsicum, onion and tomato into chunky pieces. On a wooden skewer push on a piece of capsicum, onion, tomato, one each of the three pieces of chicken kebab and repeat with the vegetables. Barbecue over an open flame and drizzle with oil or ghee while cooking. To serve, add the butter to the couscous and reheat until it melts. Serve the kebabs on a bed of couscous. Serve with cucumber raita.

FOR THE COUSCOUS
250 ml (8 fl oz/1 cup) water
1 teaspoon oil
175 g (6 oz/1 cup) couscous
20 g (¾ oz) butter
1 green capsicum (bell pepper)
1 Spanish (Bermuda) onion
1 tomato
Oil or ghee, for drizzling
Salt
Cucumber Raita (see recipe), to serve

Curried Potato with Caramelised Onion Purée

Every region of India has a different way of making potato curry. I have added coconut milk to it. Since this is a quintessential southern Indian ingredient my potato curry is southern. The caramelised onion purée, with its sweet flavour complements the spicy potatoes. Serve with roti or naan bread.

Serves: 2 / Preparation time: 15 minutes / Cooking time: 40 minutes

2 potatoes, cubed
1 tablespoon vegetable oil
½ teaspoon mustard seeds
½ teaspoon turmeric
6–7 curry leaves
1 onion, finely chopped
2 teaspoons tomato paste
2 teaspoons curry powder
120 ml (4 fl oz/½ cup) coconut milk
½ teaspoon salt
½ teaspoon sugar
250 ml (8 fl oz/1 cup) water

FOR THE CARAMELISED
ONION PURÉE
50 g (1¾ oz) butter
2 onions, sliced
⅛ teaspoon salt
120 ml (4 fl oz/½ cup) milk, warmed

Boil the potatoes in a large pan of water over medium heat for 20 minutes, or until tender. Heat the oil in a saucepan and sauté the mustard seeds, turmeric and curry leaves until the mustard seeds pop. Add the onion and sauté until translucent and then add the tomato paste. Add the curry powder, coconut milk, potatoes, salt, sugar and water. Turn the heat to medium-low and cook with a lid on for 15–20 minutes, or until the potatoes are soft. Reduce the sauce until it thickens.

Meanwhile, to make the caramelised onion purée, heat the butter in a saucepan and add the sliced onion. Sauté the onions over medium heat for 3–5 minutes, or until they turn golden brown and then add salt. Transfer the onions to a blender with the warm milk and blend until a smooth purée.

Serve the potatoes on a bed of onion purée.

Chettinad Chicken with Aloo Gobi and Pear Chutney

Chettinad is a region in the Tamil Nadu state in South India. The region is famous for its cuisine, specifically Chettinad chicken. The poultry is poached in stock for 30 minutes, which keeps the meat moist and flavourful.

Serves: 2 / Preparation time: 20 minutes / Cooking time: 40 minutes

1 kg (2¼ lb) whole chicken
2 tablespoons vegetable oil
2 cm (¾ in) piece of root ginger
4 garlic cloves
5–7 curry leaves
2 onions, diced
½ tablespoon poppy seeds
1 teaspoon coriander seeds
1 teaspoon cumin seeds
1 star anise
2 red chillies
1 cinnamon quill (stick)
3 cardamon pods
2 cloves
1 tomato, diced
1 litre (1 ¾ pints) water or chicken stock
⅛ teaspoon salt
2 teaspoons sugar
Juice of ½ lemon
120 ml (4 fl oz/½ cup) coconut milk

Remove the legs, wings and thighs of the chicken and set aside.

Heat the oil in a large pan and add the ginger and garlic and sauté for 1 minute. Add the curry leaves and onion and sauté for 3–5 minutes, or until the onions are translucent. Add the seeds and spices and cook for 1 minute, or until fragrant. Add the tomato and sauté for another 2 minutes. Add the water or stock and salt and bring to the boil. Turn the heat off, lower the chicken into the stock and leave covered for 30 minutes.

Remove the chicken from the pan and set aside. Add the sugar, lemon juice and coconut milk to the stock and reduce the sauce over medium heat until it thickens. Blend the sauce to a fine purée using a blender. Debone the breast from the chicken.

FOR THE ALOO GOBI

½ litre (17 fl oz) vegetable oil
1 large potato, diced
50 g (1¾ oz) cauliflower, cut into
small florets
Salt, to taste
½ teaspoon ground cumin
½ teaspoon ground coriander

FOR THE PEAR CHUTNEY

1 tablespoon vegetable oil
2 eschalots
½ teaspoon cumin seeds
½ teaspoon coriander seeds
1 pear, diced
2 tablespoons caster (superfine) sugar
⅛ teaspoon salt
250 ml (8 fl oz/1 cup) water

To make the aloo gobi, heat the vegetable oil in a saucepan and deep fry the potatoes and cauliflower for 5 minutes. Once the vegetables are golden brown and crispy, drain on kitchen paper and sprinkle with salt, ground cumin and ground coriander. Set aside.

To make the pear chutney, heat 1 tablespoon oil in a saucepan over medium heat. Sauté the eschalots for 2 minutes until translucent, then add the cumin and coriander seeds, pear, sugar, salt and water. Bring to the boil and reduce the heat to a simmer. Cook for 20 minutes, or until the pears are very tender, and the liquid has evaporated. Set aside to cool. Pile the aloo gobi on a plate and place chicken over the aloo gobi. Drizzle the sauce around the chicken on the plate.

Chicken Cafreal Wings Served with Cucumber, Baby Tomato and Baby Pea Sprout Salad

The chillies and coriander give deep green colour to the juicy finger-licking chicken wings. Black peppercorns, cumin and coriander provide a spice hit and the cucumber salad accompaniment is cooling.

Serves: 4 / Preparation time: 15 minutes / Cooking time: 30 minutes

1 bunch fresh coriander (cilantro)
4 green chillies
4 cm (1¾ in) piece of root ginger
4 garlic cloves
10 black peppercorns
½ cinnamon quill (stick)
1 teaspoon cumin seeds
1 teaspoon turmeric
Juice of 1 lime
15 g (½ oz) tamarind or 1 tablespoon tamarind paste
2 teaspoon sugar
½ teaspoon salt
50 ml (2 fl oz/¼ cup) water
600 g (1 lb 6 oz) chicken wings
Oil, for drizzling

FOR THE SALAD
2 Lebanese cucumbers
100 g (3½ oz) baby tomatoes
20 g (¾ oz) green pea sprouts
1 teaspoon sugar
2 tablespoons balsamic vinegar
⅛ teaspoon salt
Cracked black pepper
2 tablespoons olive oil

Make a paste using the coriander, chillies, ginger, garlic, peppercorns, cinnamon, cumin seeds, turmeric, sugar, lime, tamarind, salt and water using a blender and process until smooth.

Put the chicken wings in a non-metallic dish and brush the marinade over. Marinate for at least 2 hours and refrigerate.

Preheat the oven to 180°C/350°F/Gas mark 4. Transfer the chicken wings to a baking sheet lined with baking paper. Drizzle a little oil over the chicken and bake for 20–25 minutes, or until tender. Baste the chicken with the liquid from the baking sheet.

Meanwhile, to make the salad, peel and dice the cucumbers, halve the tomatoes and chop the pea sprouts.

Prepare the dressing by whisking the sugar, balsamic vinegar, salt, pepper and olive oil in a bowl. Drizzle over the salad and toss together just before serving. Serve the salad with chicken wings.

Mangalore Squid Masala with Dosai

The Konkan region on the western coast of India stretches from Maharashtra to Kerala through Mangalore. The cuisine varies as you move south through the Konkan belt. Mangalore cuisine or Udupi cuisine places dosai at the centre of the meal. As Mangalore is on the coastal part of India it also relies a lot on seafood.

Serves: 2 / Preparation time: 10 minutes (if using packed or prepared dosai mix) / Cooking time: 15 minutes

Combine the chilli powder, turmeric, ground cumin and ground coriander with the vinegar in a small bowl and make a paste. Set aside.

In a wok, heat the vegetable oil over medium heat, sauté the mustard seeds and curry leaves until the mustard seeds pop. Add the onion and sauté for 2 minutes, or until translucent. Add the curry paste and sauté for another 20 seconds. Add the squid rings and cook for 1 minute, then add the salt and sugar and toss in the wok.

Arrange the squid in one half of the dosai and fold the other half over to make a sandwich.

1 teaspoon red chilli powder
¼ teaspoon turmeric
1 teaspoon ground cumin
1 teaspoon ground coriander
1 tablespoon white wine vinegar
2 tablespoons vegetable oil
¼ teaspoon mustard seeds
Handful of curry leaves
1 onion, finely chopped
1 squid, cut into rings
⅛ teaspoon salt
½ teaspoon sugar
Dosai (see recipe), to serve

Bisi Bele Hulianna Karnataka Risotto

Bisi bele hulianna translated from the Kannada language means 'hot lentil sour rice'. This is no ordinary risotto, it is packed full of flavours. The combination of red chillies, lentils, split yellow peas and fenugreek seeds make it distinctly south Indian.

Serves: 4 / Preparation time: 15 minutes / Cooking time: 40 minutes

Dry roast all the hulianna spice mix ingredients for 2–3 minutes, or until fragrant, then blend to a fine powder in a mortar and using a pestle.

Preheat the oven to 180°C/350°F/Gas mark 4. Dice the pumpkin, place on a baking sheet, drizzle over a little oil and roast in the oven for 10–12 minutes, or until tender.

Melt the butter in a saucepan and sauté the finely chopped leek for 2 minutes, or until translucent. Add the red chilli and curry leaves and sauté them for another 1 minute. Add the arborio rice and peanuts and sauté for 1 minute, then add 1 tablespoon of hulianna spice mix and the curry powder. Add the stock, 150 ml (¼ pint/²/₃ cup) at a time, waiting until it is absorbed before adding the next batch. Just before the rice is al dente, add the tomato, pumpkin, peas, tamarind paste and salt. Serve with shev.

100 g (3½ oz) pumpkin
1 teaspoon vegetable oil, for drizzling
30 g (1 oz) butter
1 leek, finely chopped
1 red chilli, finely chopped
5–6 curry leaves
200 g (7 oz/1 cup) arborio rice
1 tablespoon raw peanuts
2 teaspoons curry powder
1 litre (1¾ pints) vegetable stock
1 tomato, diced
55 g (2 oz/½ cup) frozen peas
1 teaspoon tamarind paste
⅛ teaspoon salt
Shev (crispy chickpea noodles), to serve

FOR THE HULIANNA SPICE MIX
50 g (1¾ oz) yellow dried split peas
2 tablespoons urid dal (black or white lentils)
4 green cardamom pods
4 cloves
1 teaspoon cumin seeds
1 teaspoon fenugreek seeds
1 cinnamon quill (stick)
2 dry red chillies

Rogan Gosht Spiced Lamb with Onion Fritters and Spiced Jus

Rogan gosht or josh originates from Kashmir. The Kashmiri chillies give the dish its red colour and the spice. Traditionally rogan gosht is slow cooked with goat pieces but I have used lamb cutlet to make the recipe suitable for cooking quickly. Serve with vegetable pilaf.

Serves: 1 / Preparation time: 20 minutes / Cooking time: 30 minutes

Dry roast the fennel seeds, cinnamon, saffron and cumin seeds for 2–3 minutes, or until fragrant and blend into fine powder using a mortar and pestle. Combine the powdered spices with the ground ginger, chilli powder, mace and salt.

Using a sharp knife, remove the eye fillets, or the meat, from the lamb cutlets leaving the bone behind. Heat 1 tablespoon of the ghee in a saucepan and add 2 black cardamom pods. Sear the lamb cutlets on both sides for 30 seconds. Remove from the pan and roll them in the spice mix to coat evenly, then cook in the pan for another 30 seconds. Remove the lamb from the pan, loosely cover with aluminium foil and leave to rest for 5 minutes.

To make jus, put the rest of the ghee and cardamom in a saucepan with ¼ teaspoon of the spice mix and the chicken stock. Heat until the stock is reduced by half, or until thick, then add the butter and stir until dissolved.

To make the onion fritters, heat the vegetable oil in a large heavy pan. Meanwhile, slice the onion into thin rounds and combine in a bowl with the flour, salt, turmeric, chilli powder, water and ice cubes. Deep fry 1 onion slice at a time until golden brown.

On a plate, arrange the lamb fillets so they are next to each other, and drizzle over the jus. Place the onion fritters and scoop vegetable pilaf besides the fritters.

½ teaspoon fennel seeds
1 cinnamon quill (stick)
3 saffron strands
½ teaspoon cumin seeds
½ teaspoon ground ginger
½ teaspoon chilli powder
½ teaspoon mace
¼ teaspoon salt
2 lamb cutlets
2 tablespoons ghee
4 black cardamom pods
250 ml (8 fl oz/1 cup) chicken stock
15 g (½ oz) butter
Vegetable pilaf (see recipe), to serve

FOR THE ONION FRITTERS
Vegetable oil, for deep frying
1 medium onion
85 g (3 oz/¾ cup) plain (all-purpose)
   flour
¼ teaspoon salt
¼ teaspoon turmeric
¼ teaspoon chilli powder
250 ml (8 fl oz/1 cup) water
4–5 ice cubes

Slow-cooked Kolhapuri Goat with Cauliflower Purée and Papadums

This is my signature dish and it's inspired by my hometown of Kolhapur, which has a reputation for excellent goat meat. Traditionally, this recipe is cooked in a clay pot over open fire. The spicy goat combines well with the sweet cauliflower purée and melts in the mouth. Use the crunchy papadums to scoop up the tender meat.

Serves: 4 / Preparation time: 20 minutes / Cooking time: 2 hours 30 minutes

2 tablespoons vegetable oil
2 tablespoons natural (plain) yogurt
500 g (1 lb 2 oz) goat shoulder, diced
2 teaspoons salt
20 g (¾ oz) green pea sprouts, to garnish
Papadums, to serve

FOR THE CURRY PASTE
1 onion, finely chopped
1 teaspoon oil
Handful of fresh coriander (cilantro)
½ teaspoon coriander seeds
½ teaspoon cumin seeds
4 garlic cloves
2 cm (¾ in) piece of root ginger
1 teaspoon tomato paste
½ teaspoon turmeric
1 teaspoon chilli powder
1 teaspoon garam masala

FOR THE CAULIflOWER PURÉE
1 teaspoon butter
¼ cauliflower, coarsely chopped
¼ teaspoon turmeric
150 ml (¼ pint/⅔ cup) thickened (double, heavy) cream
½ teaspoon salt
½ teaspoon ground cumin
½ teaspoon ground coriander
1 teaspoon lemon juice

Preheat the oven to 160°C/325°F/Gas mark 3.

To make the curry paste, sauté the onion until golden brown in a frying pan over medium heat with 1 teaspoon oil. Add in the rest of the curry ingredients, sauté for 3–4 minutes and transfer to a blender. Blend to a fine paste.

Heat the 2 tablespoons of vegetable oil in an ovenproof casserole over medium heat and sauté the curry paste for 5 minutes, or until the oil starts separating. Add the yogurt and sauté for another 1 minute, then add the meat and sauté for another 2 minutes. Add the salt and 250 ml (8 fl oz/1 cup) of water, stir and cover with a lid, then bake for at least 2 hours, or until the lamb is tender and shreds easily. Check every 30 minutes and add more water, if necessary. Shred the lamb in the sauce and mix thoroughly.

To make the cauliflower purée, melt the butter in a saucepan over medium heat. Add the cauliflower and turmeric and sauté for 2 minutes. Add the cream and cook, stirring occasionally, for 10 minutes until the cauliflower is tender. Add the salt, cumin and coriander powder and lemon juice and leave to cool. Blend the cold mixture to a fine purée.

To serve, reheat the cauliflower purée, smear it on a plate. Add the shredded lamb and put roasted papadums on the side. Garnish with pea sprouts.

Tandoori-spiced Spatchcock with Pickled Onion

Spatchcock is both a method of cooking chicken and also a name for juvenile chicken. This dish is a reinvention of tandoori chicken. Pickled onions are traditionally served with tandoori chicken as it breaks down the heat from the spices.

Serves: 2 / Preparation time: 20 minutes / Cooking time: 40 minutes

1 spatchcock, approximately 500 g (1 lb 2 oz)
Cucumber Raita (see recipe), to serve

FOR THE PICKLE
1 Spanish (Bermuda) onion
¼ teaspoon red chilli powder
120 ml (4 fl oz/½ cup) white vinegar
2 teaspoons sugar
¼ teaspoon salt

FOR THE TANDOORI PASTE
½ teaspoon turmeric
1 teaspoon red chilli powder
½ teaspoon curry powder
2 garlic cloves
2 cm (¾ in) piece of root ginger
Juice of 1 lemon
1 teaspoon sugar

FOR THE JUS
40 g (1½ oz) butter
1 teaspoon plain (natural) yogurt
250 ml (8 fl oz/1 cup) water
1 teaspoon sugar
⅛ teaspoon salt

Preheat the oven to 180°C/350°F/Gas mark 4.

To make the pickle, thinly slice the onion and wash with water 2–3 times. Combine the onion with the red chilli powder in a bowl and set aside.

Bring the vinegar to the boil in a pan set over medium heat. Add the sugar and salt and boil until dissolved. Pour the hot vinegar over the sliced onions and leave to rest for at least 10 minutes.

Remove the legs and wings of the spatchcock and set aside for the jus. Debone the breast and French the wing bone, or alternatively ask your butcher to do this for you. Frenching is the process of removing all fat, meat, and connective tissue from the meat.

To make the tandoori paste, blend all the spices and sugar in a blender and mix with lemon juice. Apply quarter of the spice mix to the spatchcock breast, set on a wire rack on a baking sheet and bake in the oven for 15 minutes. Apply another quarter of the mix to the breast then cook for another 15 minutes. Remove the breast from the oven, wrap with aluminium foil and set aside to rest for 10 minutes.

Meanwhile, to make the jus, in a medium pan, melt half the butter and the rest of the spice mix and sauté for 30 seconds. Add the wings and thighs to the pan and toss through until they are coated. Add the yogurt, water, sugar and salt and cook for 5–7 minutes, or until the sauce thickens. Strain through a sieve into a clean saucepan and add the remaining butter.

Serve the spatchcock breast on a plate and drizzle with jus. Spoon the onion pickle on the plate. Serve with Cucumber Raita.

Butter-Poached Turkey with Korma Sauce and Crispy Bhujing

Turkey is known for quickly drying out while cooking. Poaching it in butter stops the drying process and makes the meat soft and moist. Bhujing is a combination of chicken and poha (rolled rice), which is native to Vasai, a small town north of Mumbai. Although turkey is not commonly cooked in India, the meat is very tasty.

Serves: 1 / Preparation time: 10 minutes / Cooking time: 40 minutes

1 teaspoon vegetable oil
1 turkey breast, 250 g (9 oz)
250 g (9 oz) unsalted butter

FOR THE KORMA SAUCE
1 tablespoon vegetable oil
2 cm (¾ in) piece of root ginger, finely chopped
4 garlic cloves, finely chopped
1 onion finely chopped
½ teaspoon turmeric
1 tomato, chopped
10 flaked almonds
20 g (¾ oz) slivered (flaked) almonds
50 ml (2 fl oz/¼ cup) yogurt
1 teaspoon red chilli powder
1 teaspoon garam masala
¼ teaspoon salt
½ teaspoon sugar

Heat the teaspoon of vegetable oil in a frying pan over medium heat and sear the turkey breast on both sides for 1 minute.

Melt the butter in a deep-sided pan until it reaches 82°C/180°F then lower the browned turkey into it. Maintain the temperature by lowering or increasing the heat and cook for 30 minutes. Take the breast out and slice diagonally into 4–5 pieces.

To make the korma sauce, heat the oil in saucepan and sauté the ginger and garlic for 30 seconds. Add onion and turmeric and sauté for 3–5 minutes, or until translucent. Add the tomato and both types of almonds, and cook until the tomatoes start to break down.

Add the yogurt, chilli powder and garam masala and cook for 3–5 minutes, or until the oil starts to separate, then add the salt and sugar. Tip the korma sauce into a blender and purée until smooth, then transfer back to the pan with 2 tablespoons of butter from the turkey poaching liquid and reheat until hot.

FOR THE BHUJING
1 teaspoon oil
¼ teaspoon mustard seeds
⅛ teaspoon turmeric
5 mm (¼ in) piece of root ginger, finely chopped
1 garlic clove, finely chopped
2 tablespoons rolled rice
⅛ teaspoon salt
½ teaspoon garam masala
1 tablespoon fresh coriander (cilantro)

Meanwhile, to make bhujing, heat the oil in a pan and sauté the mustard seeds and turmeric until the mustard seeds pop. Add finely chopped ginger and garlic and sauté for 10 seconds. Add the rolled rice, salt and the garam masala and toss for 2 minutes, or until the rice becomes crunchy. Remove from the heat and combine with chopped coriander.

Smear the korma sauce on a plate, arrange the sliced turkey and garnish with bhujing.

Pan–Seared Snapper with Malabar Masala and Avial

The Malabar region is an area from Northern Kerala, known all around the world as 'Gods Own Country'. Malabar masala and avial are native to the region and the flavours work well together. The plantain chips give crunchy texture to the dish.

Serves: 1 / Preparation time: 20 minutes / Cooking time: 30 minutes

To make the Malabar spice blend, in a frying pan, dry roast the cumin, coriander and fenugreek seeds for 2 minutes on high heat, or until fragrant. Tip into a blender. In the same pan dry-fry the curry leaves for 30 seconds, set aside, then dry-fry the coconut for 2 minutes, or until golden brown. Add both to the blender along with the chilli powder, turmeric powder and sugar and blend to a fine powder.

To make the avial, blanch all the vegetables separately in a large pan of boiling water and refresh immediately in ice cold water. Drain and transfer to a clean bowl.

Roast the cumin and coriander seeds in a frying pan and grind them in a mortar using a pestle. Mix the powder with the vegetables. Add yogurt and salt to the mix and set aside. Heat the oil in a saucepan until it smokes then turn the heat off. Add the mustard seeds and curry leaves and let the mustard seeds pop. Add the turmeric and immediately pour the oil mixture over the vegetables. Add ½ teaspoon of Malabar Spice Blend to the vegetables, mix thoroughly and set aside.

Preheat the oven to 180°C/350°F/Gas mark 4. Set aside ⅛ teaspoon of the Malabar Spice Mix and rub the rest with a little of the vegetable oil on to the fish. Heat ½ teaspoon of the oil in a frying pan until smoking and place the fish skin side down and hold it down for 20 seconds to stop from curling. Keep cooking the fish until it is cooked half way through and then transfer to the oven. Bake for 4–5 minutes, or until the top of the fish is just cooked. Remove from the oven, transfer to a clean plate and scatter over the remaining Malabar Spice Mix.

Meanwhile, heat the vegetable oil in saucepan. Remove the skin from the plantain and using a serrated peeler julienne the plantain. Deep-fry until golden brown, then transfer to kitchen paper to drain the oil. Sprinkle with salt. Serve avial along with the fish on a plate.

200 g (7 oz) snapper fillet, skin on
1 plantain (green banana)
500 ml (17 fl oz) vegetable oil, for deep frying
⅛ teaspoon salt

FOR THE MALABAR SPICE BLEND
½ teaspoon cumin seeds
½ teaspoon coriander seeds
¼ teaspoon fenugreek seeds
5–6 curry leaves
2 tablespoons desiccated (dry unsweetened shredded) coconut
¼ teaspoon chilli powder
¼ teaspoon turmeric powder
¼ teaspoon sugar

FOR THE AVIAL
30 g (1 oz) green beans
50 g (1¾ oz) pumpkin, diced
30 g (1 oz/¼ cup) green peas
50 g (1¾ oz) sweet potato, diced
30 g (1 oz) eggplant (aubergine), diced
½ teaspoon cumin seeds
½ teaspoon coriander seeds
50 ml (2 fl oz) plain (natural) yogurt
⅛ teaspoon salt
1 teaspoon vegetable oil
½ teaspoon mustard seeds
5 curry leaves
¼ teaspoon turmeric

On the Side

Side dishes are crucial to any meal not just in India but all around the world. They usually provide a different flavour profile and texture to the main dish, while complementing it. In this section I have suggested possible combinations of meats with each side dish.

Date and Tamarind Chutney

This sweet-and-sour chutney is a perfect accompaniment to samosas or aloo tikki. It is also used as a key ingredient in the famous street foods, bhel and chaat.

Preparation time: 20 minutes / Cooking time: 5 minutes

6 dates, pitted
1/8 teaspoon bicarbonate soda (baking soda)
1 tablespoon tamarind paste
2 tablespoon grated (shredded) palm sugar
1 teaspoon cumin seeds
1/8 teaspoon salt

Soak the dates with the bicarbonate of soda in a small bowl of warm water for 15 minutes.

Blend all the ingredients, including the date water in a blender and pass the chutney through a fine sieve.

Store in an airtight container for up to 2 weeks.

Peanut Chutney

A school day lunchbox favourite, this sweet and spicy chutney functions as a side dish but can also be served as a garnish with salads.

Preparation time: 5 minutes / Cooking time: 10 minutes

1/4 teaspoon vegetable oil
1/2 teaspoon cumin seeds
60 g (2 oz/1/2 cup) roasted peanuts
1 red chilli
1/2 teaspoon sugar
1 clove garlic
1/8 teaspoon salt

In a frying pan, heat the oil and sauté the cumin seeds for 30 seconds.

In a blender add all the ingredients and blend to a coarse powder.

Green Mango Chutney

Back home in India green mangoes signal the onset of summer, usually becoming available at the end of spring, which is a perfect time to make this sweet-and-sour chutney. It is perfect for serving with grilled steak or lamb.

Preparation time: 10 minutes / Cooking time: 40 minutes

2 tablespoons oil

1 tablespoon whole panchphoron

3 dried red chillies

500 g (1 lb 2 oz) green mangoes, peeled and julienned

3 medium tomatoes, deseeded and chopped

225 g (8 oz/1 cup) brown sugar

¼ teaspoon salt

1 tablespoon roasted and ground panchphoron

Heat the oil in a saucepan and add the whole panchphoron. Once the seeds start popping, add the dried chillies and sauté for 30 seconds.

Add the sliced mango and sauté for 1 minute, then add the tomatoes and sauté for another 2 minutes. Add the sugar and salt and mix well. Cover and cook for 30 minutes on medium heat, then set aside to cool.

Once cooled add the roasted and ground panchphoron. Store in an airtight container for up to 1 month.

Spicy Tomato Relish

Spicy tomato relish can provide a unique and surprising addition to the charcuterie board. It works really well with cold meats as well as traditional Indian onion fritters.

Preparation time: 10 minutes / Cooking time: 20 minutes

Heat the oil in a saucepan, and fry the onion until translucent.

Add the finely chopped chillies, garlic, ground cumin and coriander seeds and sauté for 2 minutes.

Add the tomatoes, sugar, vinegar and salt. Cover and simmer for at least 10–15 minutes, or until the tomatoes start to break down. Remove from the heat, leave to go cold and store in an airtight container.

2 tablespoons vegetable oil
1 onion, diced
2 red chillies, finely chopped
1 garlic clove, finely chopped
½ teaspoon cumin seeds
½ teaspoon coriander seeds
3 tomatoes, diced
1½ teaspoons sugar
1 tablespoon white vinegar
¼ teaspoon salt

Green Mango Relish

In the summer holidays, I used to visit my grandmother with my siblings and cousins. We used to spend entire days climbing hills and trees, and would return home clutching green mangoes, which would be turned into relish that we would savour for the entire summer. This mango relish goes really well with pork dishes.

Preparation time: Overnight / Cooking time: 10 minutes

Peel and discard the mango skin and julienne the flesh. Arrange on a plate, dust with the turmeric and salt, cover and leave overnight.

Drain the water from the mango and pat dry with kitchen paper.

In a frying pan, dry roast the fenugreek, coriander and fennel seeds, and grind in a mortar with a pestle to powder.

Mix the mango with the chilli powder, palm sugar and the powdered spice mix.

In a pan heat the oil, add the mustard seeds and fry until they pop. Turn off the heat and leave to cool.

Mix the cold oil and seeds with the mango relish mixture and store in an airtight container.

Use straight away, if you like, but for best flavour leave for 2 weeks.

500 g (1 lb 2 oz) green mango
½ teaspoon turmeric powder
100 g (3½ oz) salt
15 g (½ oz) fenugreek seeds
15 g (½ oz) coriander seeds
10 g (⅓ oz) fennel seeds
15 g (½ oz) chilli powder
120 g (4 oz) palm sugar, grated (shredded)
120 ml (4 fl oz/½ cup) vegetable oil
15 g (½ oz) mustard seeds

Preserved Lemon Relish

This is one of the most common relishes used in Indian cuisine. It is a perfect accompaniment to curried fish or parathas.

Preparation time: 10 minutes / Cooking time: 10 minutes

Heat ½ teaspoon of oil in a frying pan, then fry the fenugreek seeds until golden brown. Remove from the pan and using a mortar and pestle grind them coarsely.

Meanwhile, heat the rest of the oil in a pan and sauté the mustard seeds until they pop.

In a bowl, mix the chilli powder, turmeric, salt and add the mustard seed and oil mixture and leave to cool.

Cut each lemon into eight, add to the bowl and mix thoroughly. Store in an airtight container. The relish stays good for months.

1 tablespoon vegetable oil
1 teaspoon fenugreek seeds
1 teaspoon mustard seeds
1 teaspoon chilli powder
1 teaspoon turmeric
6 teaspoons salt
10 lemons

Cucumber Raita

Similar to Middle Eastern tatziki, cucumber raita is served as a side dish and provides much needed relief when served with a hot curry.

Preparation time: 10 minutes / Cooking time: 5 minutes

1 Lebanese cucumber
15 g (4 oz/½ cup) of plain (natural) yogurt
¼ teaspoon sugar
¼ teaspoon salt
½ teaspoon ground cumin
½ teaspoon ground coriander
1 tablespoon vegetable oil
¼ teaspoon of mustard seeds
4–5 curry leaves

Peel and discard the skin of the cucumber, then finely dice the flesh and transfer to a bowl.

Add the yogurt, sugar, salt, ground cumin and coriander to the bowl and mix well.

In a small saucepan, heat the oil until smoking, then turn the heat off. Add the mustard seeds and curry leaves and sauté until they pop. Add the oil mixture (Tadaka) to the cucumber mixture and mix thoroughly.

Drinks & desserts

I must confess I have a sweet tooth, but

sometimes traditional Indian desserts can be too sweet. In

this section, each dessert I have included contains elements

that tone down the sweet ingredient. Classic desserts

such as gulab jamun are presented alongside childhood

favourites such as panna cotta, crumble and trifle.

Masala Chai

If India had a national drink, it would be chai or tea. 'Chaiwala' or a 'Chai ki tapari' — usually a small shanty of a tea vendor are everywhere on India's streets. The kettle is constantly boiling and there is the lingering aroma of tea that's stronger than anything you've ever tasted. People meet, connect and make friends over a cuppa at the unassuming shanty.

With whole milk and sugar liberally added to the brew, chai is a perfect drink to kick-start your day. Alternatively, serve chai with shortbread at any time.

Serves: 2 / Preparation time: 5 minutes / Cooking time: 5 minutes

250 ml (8 fl oz/1 cup) milk
55 ml (2 fl oz/¼ cup) water
2 teaspoons sugar
⅛ teaspoon ground nutmeg
3 cardamom pods
1 cm (³⁄₈ in) piece of root ginger
2 teaspoons tea leaves or 4 English
breakfast tea bags

In a pan, heat the milk, water, sugar and nutmeg over a medium heat.

In a mortar and with a pestle, grind the cardamom pods and add to the milk mixture. Crush the ginger with the pestle and add to the pot.

Once the milk comes to the boil add the tea leaves and simmer for 2 minutes on low heat. Turn the heat off and leave to brew with a lid on for 1 minute. Strain into cups and serve hot.

Tip: The longer you simmer and brew, the stronger the tea tastes.

Coffee

Very popular in Southern India, this drink reminds me of my train journey around that region when the 'coffee wala' (vendor) would travel through the coaches early in the morning yelling 'kaffee'. It's impossible to resist this frothy concoction to help wake you up. Serve it after any meal.

Serves: 1 / Preparation time: 5 minutes / Cooking time: 5 minutes

Add the ground coffee to a coffee percolator. Boil the water and add to the percolator. Set aside for 3–5 minutes to brew.

Meanwhile, pour the milk, sugar and nutmeg into a pan and bring to the boil. Decant into cups.

Once the coffee is brewed, strain through a fine sieve into the hot milk.

3 teaspoons ground coffee beans
250 ml (8 fl oz/1 cup) water
250 ml (8 fl oz/1 cup) milk
1 tablespoon sugar
¼ teaspoon ground nutmeg powder

Chai Brulée with Pistachio Biscotti

Chai with biscuits (cookies) is a very common afternoon tea in India. This recipe is a reinvention of the classic dessert crème brulée with a spicy twist.

Serves 4 / Preparation time: 20 minutes / Cooking time: 20 minutes

5 green cardamom pods
2 cm (¾ in) piece of root ginger
250 ml (8 fl oz/1 cup) thickened (double or heavy) cream
250 ml (8 fl oz/1 cup) whole milk
2 teaspoons black loose tea
4 egg yolks
1 teaspoon brown sugar

FOR THE PISTACHIO BISCOTTI
100 g (3½ oz) pistachios, sliced
200 g (7 oz) plain (all-purpose) flour
180 g (6¼ oz) caster (superfine) sugar
¼ teaspoon bicarbonate of soda (baking soda)
2 eggs

Preheat the oven to 180°C/350°F/Gas mark 4. Remove the seeds from the cardamom pods and grind to a powder using a mortar and pestle. Using a pestle lightly crush the ginger.

In a saucepan, combine the cream, milk and cardamom powder, ginger and loose tea powder. Bring to the boil, then reduce the heat to low and simmer for 2 minutes.

Meanwhile, in a glass bowl, whisk the egg yolks and sugar. Strain the milk mixture and slowly pour it into the eggs while whisking on low speed.

Set the custard in the glass bowl over a large saucepan of simmering water, making sure that the base of the bowl doesn't touch the water. Using a wooden spoon, keep stirring the custard until it thickens enough to coat the back of the spoon. Pour the custard into ramekins and place in a deep ovenproof baking dish. Pour water two-thirds of the way into the baking dish, avoiding contact with the custard. Bake for 20 minutes, or until the chai brulée is just wobbly in the centre. Remove from the baking dish, leave to cool to room temperature then refrigerate for at least 2 hours.

Reduce the oven temperature to 160°C/325°F/Gas mark 3. To make the biscotti, mix all the ingredients together in a bowl until the dough comes together and form a log. Transfer to a baking sheet lined with baking paper and bake for 45–50 minutes. Remove from the oven, turn the temperature down to 140°C/275°F/Gas mark 1 and leave the biscotti to cool for 20 minutes. Bake again for another 10–15 minutes and cool on a wire rack.

Remove the brulée from the refrigerator and dust with brown sugar. Caramelise the sugar using a cook's blow torch or under the grill (broiler). Serve with 2 or 3 slices of biscotti.

Shrikhand with Glazed Raspberries and Pistachio and Besan Crumble

'Shrikhand' meaning 'hung yogurt' originates from Maharashtra. Yogurt is hung overnight tied up in a muslin cloth. It is then mixed with sugar and saffron. The besan crumble provides a slightly crunchy texture to the soft shrikhand.

Serves: 6 / Preparation time: Overnight / Cooking time: 20 minutes

1 kg (2 lb 4 oz) Greek (strained plain) yogurt
5 cardamom pods
120 ml (4 fl oz/½ cup) milk
10 saffron strands
250 ml (8 fl oz/1 cup) caster (superfine) sugar

FOR THE GLAZED RASPBERRIES
10 g (⅓ oz) caster (superfine) sugar
2 teaspoons water
30 g (1 oz) unsalted butter
250 g (9 oz) raspberries

FOR THE PISTACHIO AND BESAN CRUMBLE
55 g (2 oz/½ cup) pistachio nuts
115 g (4 oz/1 cup) besan or chickpea (gram) flour
55 g (2 oz/½ cup) butter, diced
55 g (2 oz/½ cup) brown sugar

Pour the yogurt into a muslin cloth and tie it tightly with kitchen string. Hang it overnight to let all the water drain out.

Meanwhile, remove the seeds from the cardamom pods and pound them into powder in a mortar using a pestle. In a saucepan, bring the milk and saffron to the boil, reduce the temperature and simmer for 3 minutes.

In a food processor, mix the strained yogurt, cardamom powder, sugar and saffron milk until smooth. Transfer to a bowl and refrigerate.

Preheat the oven to 180°C/350°F/Gas mark 4.

To make the glazed raspberries, dissolve the sugar in the water over low heat in a saucepan, add the butter and reduce the liquid to make a thick sauce. Put the raspberries in a bowl, pour over the sauce and refrigerate until needed.

To make the crumble, blend the pistachio nuts, besan flour, butter and sugar in a food processor until the mixture resembles fine breadcrumbs. Transfer to a baking sheet and bake for 10–15 minutes, or until golden brown.

To assemble, part fill a bowl with the yogurt, top with raspberries and crumble. Serve chilled.

Rice Pudding Topped with Fresh Mango, Candied Almonds, Tuile and Mango Coolie

Rice puddings are found in nearly all areas of the world. The methods of cooking vary by region. In India the rice is slowly cooked in milk and spices. Served hot or cold, this pudding is delicious. The mango cuts through the sweetness of the pudding, and the candied almonds and tuile provide crunchy texture to the dish.

Serves: 2 / Preparation time 10 minutes / Cooking time: 20 minutes

2 tablespoons medium grain rice
750 ml (1¼ pints/3 cups) milk
115 g (4 oz /½ cup) sugar
¼ teaspoon cardamom powder

FOR THE MANGO COOLIE
1 mango
250 ml (8 fl oz/1 cup) water
2 tablespoons sugar
1 cinnamon quill (stick)
1 star anise

FOR THE CANDIED ALMONDS
1 teaspoon sugar
2 teaspoons water
1 teaspoon slivered (flaked) almonds
⅛ teaspoon salt

FOR THE TUILE
50 g (1¾ oz) icing (confectioners') sugar
50 g (1¾ oz) plain (all-purpose) flour
60 g (2 oz) egg white (approximately 1 egg white)
30 g (1 oz) butter, melted

Put the rice, milk, sugar and cardamom in a pan, bring to the boil, reduce the temperature to low and cook slowly for 15–20 minutes, or until the pudding is thick.

To make the mango coolie, slice half of the mango and set aside. Remove the seed and make a pulp by blending the rest of the mango in a blender. Pour the water, sugar, cinnamon, star anise and mango pulp into a saucepan, place over medium heat and simmer until the coolie reduces to a thick glossy liquid. Leave to go cold, then refrigerate.

Preheat the oven to 180°C/350°F/Gas mark 4.

To make the candied almonds, heat the sugar and water in a small saucepan until the sugar dissolves. When the sugar starts to caramelise, remove from the heat and let the bubbles subside. Add the almonds and salt, pour onto a baking sheet lined with baking paper and let it cool until it becomes hard.

To make the tuile, combine all the ingredients in a bowl and using a spatula, thinly spread on a baking sheet lined with baking paper. Bake for 5–6 minutes, or until it starts to turn golden brown. Remove from the oven and shape, before it cools, into triangles, using a knife.

Scoop out the pudding using a measuring cup and arrange on a plate. Place the sliced mango on top, drizzle over the coolie and place the tuile in the pudding and the candied almonds scattered over.

Gulab Jamun with Orange Marmalade, Vanilla Ice Cream and Pistachio Praline

Gulab jamun is a popular Indian dessert. Traditionally, it is served with sugar syrup but I think it works really well with ice cream, which cuts through the sweetness of the gulab jamun. Make the ice cream using an ice cream machine, or buy your favourite brand.

Serves: 4 / Preparation time: 60 minutes / Cooking time: 40 minutes

To make the orange marmalade, put the whole oranges in a large saucepan, cover with water and put a lid on. Bring to the boil, then simmer for 1 hour, until soft. Remove the oranges with a slotted spoon and set aside until cool. Continue to reduce the cooking liquid by heating it until it measures 75 ml (2½ fl oz/¹/₃ cup). Peel the cold oranges, discard the pips, but set aside the peel, then purée the flesh in a food processor or blender. Strain the purée and add it to the cooking liquid. Finely shred the peel and add it to the cooking liquid with the sugar. Bring to the boil and reduce the heat. Cook for 5–10 minutes or until it achieves a syrupy consistency, stirring frequently.

To make the ice cream, remove the seeds from the vanilla bean. Heat the milk in a saucepan and add the seeds and pod. Bring to the boil, then strain into a mixing bowl.

In another bowl, whisk the egg yolks with the sugar until the mixture is a pale yellow colour. Pour the hot milk on the egg mixture while stirring to avoid the eggs scrambling. Set the bowl over a pan of boiling water, so that the base of the bowl doesn't come into contact with the water and cook the custard while stirring until it coats the back of the spoon. Let it cool and once cooled, churn in an ice cream machine.

FOR THE ORANGE MARMALADE
500 g (1 lb 2 oz) oranges
300 g (11 oz) caster (superfine) sugar

FOR THE VANILLA ICE CREAM
½ vanilla bean (pod)
200 ml (7 fl oz) milk
2 egg yolks
25 g (¾ oz) caster (superfine) sugar

For the gulab jamun, combine all the ingredients in a bowl and make into dough. Using your hands, flatten the dough then stamp out 4 thin round discs. Heat the oil in a saucepan on medium heat and deep fry the discs until golden brown. Set aside.

Combine the sugar syrup ingredients in a saucepan, stir and place over medium heat and continue to heat for 5–10 minutes until reduced to syrupy consistency. Soak the gulab jamuns in the sugar syrup until ready to serve.

To make the pistachio praline, heat the sugar in a saucepan over a medium heat without stirring until the sugar dissolves and the liquid turns a deep brown caramel colour. Remove from the heat and wait for the bubbles to subside, then add the pistachios. Pour the mixture onto a baking sheet lined with baking paper. Allow to cool and set hard, then break it up into shards.

On a plate, place the gulab jamun disk, add a scoop of ice cream on top, drizzle sugar syrup over, then add a teaspoon of marmalade and insert the praline shard in the ice cream.

FOR THE GULAB JAMUN
115 g (4 oz/1 cup) milk powder
45 g (1½ oz/⅓ cup) plain (all-purpose) flour
75 ml (2½ fl oz/⅓ cup) plain (natural) yogurt
⅓ teaspoon baking powder
1 tablespoon ghee
500 ml (17 fl oz) oil, for deep frying

FOR THE SUGAR SYRUP
250 g (9 oz) caster (superfine) sugar
350 ml (12 fl oz/1½ cups) water
10–12 saffron strands
½ teaspoon orange blossom water
½ teaspoon rose water

FOR THE PISTACHIO PRALINE
100 g (3½ oz) caster (superfine) sugar
55g (2 oz) pistachio nuts

Semolina Halva

Halva means sweet. Semolina halva is prevalent in India, Afghanistan, Nepal, Bangladesh, Pakistan and surrounding countries, and is also found in Albania, Azerbaijan, Bulgaria, Cyprus, Greece, Montenegro, Macedonia and Turkey. The texture of the halva is soft so it needs something crunchy to complement. I have used blueberries, which provide freshness and a bit of tang when you bite into them.

Serves: 1 / Preparation time: 10 minutes / Cooking time: 10 minutes

Heat the ghee or butter in a saucepan and add the semolina, toast over medium heat for 3–5 minutes, or until golden brown, stirring constantly. Add the milk and 3 tablespoons of sugar, cover with a lid and cook over low heat for 2 minutes. The semolina will double in size and turn fluffy.

In a bowl, dissolve the remaining sugar in the cream using a spoon and set aside.

Serve the semolina halva on a plate, drizzle with cream, scatter over blueberries and garnish with basil.

1 tablespoon ghee or butter
40 g (1½ oz/¼ cup) fine semolina
125 ml (4 fl oz/½ cup) milk
3 tablespoons sugar
75 ml (2½ fl oz/⅓ cup) cream
2 teaspoons sugar
30 g (1 oz) blueberries
Asian or holy basil leaves

Mum's Trifle

Trifle is my favourite dessert. My mum makes excellent trifle and still makes it when I visit her back in India. I also learned how to make classic British trifle from Heston with off course a Heston touch. So in my recipe, I have tried to incorporate the best of both worlds.

Serves: 4 / Preparation time: 30 minutes / Cooking time: 2 hours

Put the halved strawberries in a saucepan with the butter, sugar, orange blossom and rose waters and cook for 20–25 minutes, or until thick and syrupy. Divide between 4 serving glasses, leave to go cold, then refrigerate.

Preheat the oven to 180°C/350°F/Gas mark 4.

To make the custard, in a heatproof bowl, whisk the sugar and egg yolk together. In a saucepan, combine the milk, vanilla and saffron and bring to the boil. Strain through a sieve and whisk into the egg mixture. Set the bowl over a pan of gently simmering water and stir the custard until it reaches 82°C/180°F, or until it coats the back of a wooden spoon. Set aside to cool. Divide the custard between the glasses.

To make the trifle base, pound the cookies to crumbs in a bowl and mix with the melted butter and icing sugar. Place on a baking sheet and bake for 10–12 minutes, or until golden brown. Spread the baked crumbs over the custard.

Whip the cream and sugar in a mixing bowl until soft peaks form, then pipe the cream over the crumb. Garnish with fresh raspberries and dust with icing sugar.

250 g (9 oz) fresh strawberries, halved
30 g (1 oz) unsalted butter
20 g (¾ oz) caster (superfine) sugar
1 teaspoon orange blossom water
1 teaspoon rose water
125 g (4½ oz) fresh raspberries, to decorate
Icing (confectioners') sugar, for dusting

FOR THE CUSTARD
15 g (½ oz) sugar
1 egg yolk
100 ml (3½ fl oz) milk
½ vanilla bean (pod)
10 saffron strands

FOR THE TRIfLE BASE
3 Marie (rich tea) biscuits (cookies)
20 g (¾ oz) unsalted butter, melted
2 teaspoons icing (confectioners') sugar

FOR THE CHANTILLY CREAM
100 ml (3½ fl oz) thickened (double or heavy) cream
20 g (¾ oz) sugar

Mango Panna Cotta with Candied Mango

Panna cotta is a mix of sugar and cream and by flavouring the cream it's possible to change the taste of the dessert. Panna cotta should be slightly wobbly in the centre. Mango is India's national fruit. The gelatine sets the panna cotta quickly. Vegetarians can use agar agar in its place.

Serves: 2 / Preparation time: 10 minutes / Cooking time: 30 minutes

1 gelatine leaf (gold strength) or 4 g agar agar
150 ml (¼ pint/⅔ cup) cream
50 ml (2 fl oz) mango pulp
30 g (1 oz) sugar

FOR THE CANDIED MANGO
140 g (4½ oz) mango flesh
30 g (1 oz) brown sugar
1 cinnamon quill (stick)
1 star anise
1 tablespoon water

Soak the gelatine leaf in a small bowl of ice cold water for 2–3 minutes.

In a saucepan combine the cream, mango pulp and sugar and bring to the boil. Squeeze the softened gelatine leaf, then dissolve it in the milk. Strain into a mould and leave to cool before refrigerating.

Meanwhile, in a saucepan, combine the mango, sugar, cinnamon, star anise and water and bring it to the boil. Reduce the heat and simmer for 10 minutes until it thickens.

Serve the panna cotta with candied mango on top.

Honey Parfait, Guava Pudding, Tapioca Pearls and Candied Pineapple

Guavas are an under-appreciated fruit and when combined with honey they are a match made in heaven. Red pulp guavas are sweeter than white. There are lot of different textures at play in this dish, including frozen parfait, soft guava pudding, sticky tapioca pearls and crunchy pineapple.

Serves: 2 / Preparation time: 30 minutes / Cooking time: 40 minutes

100 ml (4 fl oz/½ cup) guava juice
½ fresh guava, seeds removed
2 tablespoons sugar
2 teaspoons rum

FOR THE HONEY PARFAIT
40 g (1¼ oz) honey
2 egg yolks
150 ml (¼ pint/⅔ cup) thickened
(heavy or double) cream

FOR THE TAPIOCA PEARLS
1 tablespoon tapioca
50 ml (2 fl oz/¼ cup) milk
2 teaspoons sugar
Zest of ¼ lime

FOR THE CANDIED PINEAPPLE
1 canned pineapple ring, sliced, plus
50 ml (2 fl oz/¼ cup) juice from
the can
2 tablespoons sugar
2 tablespoons golden (light corn)
syrup

Soak the tapioca in a small bowl of water for at least 30 minutes.

In a saucepan, combine the guava juice with the sugar and bring to the boil. Dice the guava into 1 cm (3/8 in) cubes. Add it to the guava juice and cook for 4–5 minutes, or until the guava is tender. Add the rum and set aside to cool.

Meanwhile, to make the honey parfait, heat the honey in a saucepan. In a bowl, whisk the egg yolks until pale, then pour the honey in a thin stream into the egg yolks while whisking constantly. In another bowl, whip the cream until soft peaks form and fold into the honey and egg mixture. Pour into separate ramekins lined with cling film (plastic wrap).

To make the tapioca pearls, add the milk, sugar, soaked tapioca and lime zest to a pan, place over medium heat and cook for 3–5 minutes, or until the mixture thickens.

To make candied pineapple, heat the pineapple juice, sugar and golden syrup in a saucepan. Add the sliced pineapple and cook for 2–3 minutes, or until golden and sticky.

Remove the honey parfait from the ramekins, place it on a plate. Spoon the guava pudding on top of the parfait, then the tapioca pearls. Place the candied pineapples on the side.

Apple and Cranberry Crumble with Kulfi

Good old English crumble is often served with vanilla ice cream. Kulfi is the ice cream of India. It is made without the addition of egg making it suitable for vegans. Kulfi needs to be made in an ice cream machine unless you can get your hands on store-made kulfi.

Serves: 4 / Preparation time: 15 minutes / Cooking time: 50 minute

3 hard eating apples, peeled, cored and sliced
55 g (2 oz/¼ cup) packed brown sugar
20 g (¾ oz) unsalted butter
1 cinnamon quill (stick)
3 cardamom pods
Zest of ½ lemon
45 g (1½ oz/⅓ cup) dried cranberries

FOR THE KULfi
500 ml (17 fl oz) whole milk
200 ml (7 fl oz) sweetened condensed milk
115 g (4 oz/½ cup) sugar
115 g (4 oz/½ cup) milk powder
½ teaspoon cardamom powder
30 g (1 oz/¼ cup) roasted crushed pistachios

FOR THE CRUMBLE
½ tablespoon brown sugar
60 g (2¼ oz) plain (all-purpose) flour
50 g (1¾ oz) rolled oats
2 tablespoons pistachios, crushed
50 g (1¾ oz) unsalted butter, chilled

To make the kulfi, combine the milk, condensed milk, sugar and milk powder in a pan and bring to a simmer over low heat. Heat until reduced to a quarter of the initial volume, then leave to cool. Add the cardamom powder and crushed pistachios. Churn in an ice cream machine according to the manufacturer's instructions.

Preheat the oven to 180°C/350°F/Gas mark 4.

Meanwhile, in a saucepan, combine the apples with the sugar, butter, cinnamon, cardamom, lemon zest and dried cranberries and simmer over medium heat for 20 minutes, or until the apples are tender but still holding their shape. Divide into two 8–10 cm (3–4 in) baking dishes.

To make the crumble, combine the sugar, flour, oats and crushed pistachios in a bowl, then grate (shred) the chilled butter into the mixture. Using your fingertips, rub the butter into the flour mixture until it resembles breadcrumbs. Use to top the apple mixture, then bake for 30 minutes, or until golden brown.

Serve hot with a scoop of kulfi.

Index

Acknowledgements

My food journey has taken me to places I never imagined I'd see and helped me to foster new friendships with some amazing people. There are many people and places that inspire this book and my heartfelt gratitude goes to everyone who has been a part of this journey. Thank you for passing on the recipes and techniques, for letting me raid your kitchens and teaching me everything I know today, without holding anything back.

The place where it all began is my home in Kolhapur, India, in my mother's kitchen. Thank you Aai for breaking the mould and encouraging an inquisitive boy to cook. And to my sisters, Gouri and Punam, for always being there without any expectations. It means the world to me.

Punamtai, thank you for being that constant source of inspiration and guidance, especially on days when I was stuck in a rut.

To Era and Bipin, none of this would have been possible without you. Thank you for being there.

Thanks to Shine Australia and the entire *MasterChef* crew for giving me an opportunity to be part of the *MasterChef Australia* family and making me realise that food is where my heart is. Special thanks to Gary Mehigan, George Calombaris and Matt Preston for the support, guidance and encouragement they provided during *MasterChef*. A big thank you to New Holland Publishers for giving me this opportunity to share my modern Indian food, the entire editing crew and the spectacular photography provided by Sue Stubbs and Rhianne Contreras.

Finally, the two people I live for: to my son Sharang, staying away from you for those six months of *MasterChef* was the hardest thing I've ever done. Thank you for being so mature and patient.

To Mitra, you have been my driving force and the influence behind every success I've had since we met. Thank you my dear for challenging me to push myself out of my comfort zone, as well as for the many roles you play in my life. I couldn't have asked for a better partner to share this adventure with.